CW01336008

Morality from Compassion

INGMAR PERSSON

OXFORD
UNIVERSITY PRESS

OXFORD
UNIVERSITY PRESS

Great Clarendon Street, Oxford, OX2 6DP,
United Kingdom

Oxford University Press is a department of the University of Oxford.
It furthers the University's objective of excellence in research, scholarship,
and education by publishing worldwide. Oxford is a registered trade mark of
Oxford University Press in the UK and in certain other countries

© Ingmar Persson 2021

The moral rights of the author have been asserted

First Edition published in 2021

Impression: 1

All rights reserved. No part of this publication may be reproduced, stored in
a retrieval system, or transmitted, in any form or by any means, without the
prior permission in writing of Oxford University Press, or as expressly permitted
by law, by licence or under terms agreed with the appropriate reprographics
rights organization. Enquiries concerning reproduction outside the scope of the
above should be sent to the Rights Department, Oxford University Press, at the
address above

You must not circulate this work in any other form
and you must impose this same condition on any acquirer

Published in the United States of America by Oxford University Press
198 Madison Avenue, New York, NY 10016, United States of America

British Library Cataloguing in Publication Data
Data available

Library of Congress Control Number: 2021935196

ISBN 978–0–19–284553–5

DOI: 10.1093/oso/9780192845535.001.0001

Printed and bound in Great Britain by
Clays Ltd, Elcograf S.p.A.

Links to third party websites are provided by Oxford in good faith and
for information only. Oxford disclaims any responsibility for the materials
contained in any third party website referenced in this work.

Contents

Acknowledgements — vii

1. Schopenhauer on Compassion as the Basis of Morality — 1
   1.1 Morality Based on Compassion by an Empirical Method — 1
   1.2 Compassion and Other Moral Attitudes Based on Empathy — 7
   1.3 Moral versus Anti-Moral Attitudes — 17
   1.4 Justice-Based Attitudes — 22
   1.5 The Aim of This Book — 25

2. Morality and the Distinction between Oneself and Others — 31
   2.1 An Ambiguity in Parfit's View — 31
   2.2 Well-Being Accessed from the Inside and the Outside — 35
   2.3 Reasons of Justice, and Coexisters — 47
   2.4 Schopenhauer on the Metaphysics of Compassion — 55

3. The Partiality and Moral Importance of Empathy — 67
   3.1 Bloom and Prinz' Attack on the Moral Importance of Empathy — 67
   3.2 Spontaneous Empathy and Voluntary, Reflective Empathy — 76
   3.3 Further Objections to the Moral Importance of Empathy — 85
   3.4 Morality and Self-Renunciation — 93

4. Biases in Favour of the Negative — 107
   4.1 Negativity Biases and Negatively Weighted Utilitarianism — 107
   4.2 Compassion as the Source of the Strict Negativity Bias — 117
   4.3 The Negativity Bias and Prioritarianism versus Egalitarianism — 122

5. Demandingness as an Objection to Norms — 125

References — 139
Index — 143

Acknowledgements

Chapter 2 partly derives from section 1 of my 'Parfit's Reorientation: From Revisionism to Conciliationalism' in Jeff McMahan, Tim Campbell, James Goodrich, and Ketan Ramakrishnan, eds., *Principles and Persons: The Legacy of Derek Parfit* (Oxford University Press, 2021), and 3.1–3.3 build on Ingmar Persson and Julian Savulescu: 'The Moral Importance of Reflective Empathy', *Neuroethics*, 11 (2018), 183–93. I am grateful to OUP's readers for comments that have led to significant improvements and, especially, to Peter Momtchiloff for being the kind of editor every author would wish to have. Finally, I would like to express my gratitude to the Uehiro Foundation for Ethics and Education for generously providing financial and academic support through the Oxford Uehiro Centre for Practical Ethics.

1
Schopenhauer on Compassion as the Basis of Morality

1.1 Morality Based on Compassion by an Empirical Method

Arthur Schopenhauer proposes a method for laying bare the basis of ethics or morality which he describes as 'empirical':

> there is no other way for discovering the foundation of ethics than the empirical, namely, to investigate whether there are generally any actions to which we must attribute *genuine moral worth*...we have to indicate the peculiar motive that moves man to actions of this kind...This motive together with the susceptibility to it will be the ultimate ground of morality... (1995: 130)

This 'empirical' method is presented as being 'diametrically opposed to Kant's' (1995: 47) method of construing morality 'as something transcendental and metaphysical, and quite independent of experience and its instruction' (1995: 50), whose basis is 'a priori knowable' (1995: 61). He sees his extensive criticism of Kant's procedure (1995: II) as 'the best preparation and guide' (1995: 47) to his own empirical procedure.[1] Morality is a set of principles or norms, and Schopenhauer's claim seems to be that we can determine what it tells us by looking at what motivates us when we are morally motivated. But this is an *empirical* method only on the dubious assumption that it is an

---

[1] As will transpire, Schopenhauer's procedure also includes an element of metaphysics, but it could still be empirical in so far as it does not postulate anything irreducibly normative as Kantian ethics seems to do.

empirical matter when we are (properly) morally motivated, what the actions are 'to which we must attribute *genuine moral worth*'.

Schopenhauer appears to assume that we can establish as a matter of empirical fact that *compassion* (*Mitleid*) is the one and only moral motive and, thus, that compassion is the basis of morality: 'Only insofar as an action has sprung from compassion does it have moral value' (1995: 144). If the motive is egoistic, it is 'consequently *without moral worth*' (1995: 143). The idea might then be that since we are morally motivated just in case compassion motivates us to relieve somebody's suffering for its own sake, this is what provides us with a moral reason to relieve somebody's suffering for its own sake. I believe that it is an empirical fact that many of us are thusly motivated, and that it is also an empirical fact that many of us *regard* this type of motivation as having moral worth. It is, however, not an empirical fact, but a matter of moral judgement that they are *correct* in so regarding it. Moreover, it is a further, quite questionable claim that compassion is commonly regarded as the *only* kind of moral motivation and that it is correct so to regard it.[2]

Schopenhauer further declares that the motive of compassion takes two forms, one of which is acting out of a sense of or concern for justice (*Gerechtigkeit*), the other which is acting out of loving-kindness or philanthropy (*Menschenliebe*): 'It is simply and solely this compassion that is the real basis of *voluntary* justice and *genuine* loving-kindness' (1995: 144). The sense of justice finds expression in the negative moral injunction 'Injure no one', and loving-kindness in the more demanding positive moral injunction 'Help everyone as much as you can':[3]

---

[2] Schopenhauer does not provide any metaethical analysis of what it means to say that a motive has moral worth, though it is to be suspected that he would favour an analysis along naturalistic lines. He stresses that 'the untutored, for whom only the concrete has meaning' (1995: 182–3) is capable of acting morally. In so far as this claim implies that agents who act out of compassion do not have to judge that their motive has moral worth in order for it to have moral worth, it is right. But he seems to overlook that to figure out what morally justified compassion would motivate you to do in a particular situation could necessitate a lot of reflection, e.g. because what he sees as two forms of compassion could conflict, as will emerge in a moment.

[3] Adam Smith (whom Schopenhauer had read) likewise speaks of 'the virtues of justice and beneficence; of which the one restrains us from hurting, and the other prompts us to promote... happiness'. These virtues are described by him as being 'originally recommended to us' 'by our benevolent affections' (1790: VI.conclusion).

> there are two clearly separate degrees wherein another's suffering can directly become my motive... In the first degree, by counteracting egoistic or malicious motives, compassion prevents me from causing suffering to another... In the second place, there is the higher degree where compassion works positively and incites me to active help. (1995: 148)

Since Schopenhauer takes egoism to be a motive without moral worth, I assume that 'no one' and 'everyone' in these moral imperatives should be understood as 'no one *else*' and 'everyone *else*'. The conjunction of the two imperatives—'the simplest and purest expression of the mode of conduct unanimously demanded by all systems of morality' (1995: 92; cf. 69–70)—would then be: 'Injure no one (else); help everyone (else) as much as you can'.

However, this imperative does not tell you what to do when you can help everyone else as much as you can only by means of injuring somebody other than yourself. So far as I can find, Schopenhauer does not deal with such complications. The closest he gets seems to be when in his extensive critique of Kantian ethics he touches on its well-known categorical imperative that exhorts us not to use human beings merely as means. He then praises it only for having the merit of indicting '*egoism* by an exceedingly characteristic sign' (1995: 97). Thus, he apparently assumes that its chief point must be to prohibit our causing *greater* harm to another in order to secure *smaller* benefits *for ourselves*. He does not consider the surely permissible exception of causing another *little* harm as a means of protecting ourselves against much greater harm, or the use of such means to protect *others* against much greater harm. Nor does he pay any attention to whether it is worse to cause such harm as a means than as a foreseen effect. Overall his attitude to this Kantian formula is disparaging and, thus, in line with his attitude to Kantian ethics in general: 'taken generally, it is inadequate, says little, and moreover is problematical' (1966: I, 349). It seems to me that Schopenhauer's treatment of this formula shows that the problem of overcoming egoism is so paramount for him that it obscures other normative issues.

If, however, he were to consider which of his two imperatives has priority, he would probably think that those with 'the higher degree' of compassion will go ahead and injure someone as a means to a greater good. According to him, goodness and badness are 'essentially relative'

(1966: I, 360; cf. 1995: 95): goodness or badness *for* someone, depending on whether it agrees or disagrees with their will. There is, however, also the total of what is good and bad for all and everyone and, as will be explained in 1.3, those with the higher degree of compassion will be acutely conscious of this total when they realize that the spatio-temporal separateness of individuals is illusory. The smaller harm inflicted on fewer beings used as a means will drown in this total value that the highly compassionate agents are motivated to make as good (or as little bad) as possible. The imperative for this moral elite would then be the consequentialist 'Injure no one else except when this is necessary to help everyone else as much as you can'. For them 'Help everyone else as much as you can' overrides 'Injure no one else'.

But for the majority of us who are morally less accomplished, it is the other way around. It is, however, implausible to outlaw all injuring of somebody else, however slight, if this is necessary for a greater good. For example, we are surely permitted to injure somebody slightly by pushing them aside when this is necessary in order to disarm a doomsday machine which would otherwise blow millions of people to pieces. Plausibly, this could be because it is a use of them as means to which they *could not reasonably object* (though they have the capacity to object reasonably). Similarly, if the injury which is necessary to help everyone as much as we can is an injury that we have to inflict on ourselves, and it would be of such a small magnitude that we could not reasonably object to it. So for these less compassionate agents the imperative would be the non-consequentialist 'Injure no one in ways to which they could reasonably object even when this is necessary to help everyone as much as you can'. These agents cannot grasp the justification for having someone, themselves or another, undergo substantial sacrifices for the greater good of everyone because their awareness of this goodness overall is insufficiently clear and lively.

There is no contradiction here because the same group of agents is not supposed to abide by both imperatives. One and the same agent cannot belong to more than one group at one period in life, that is, have compassion both in the higher degree and only in the lower degree. According to Schopenhauer's empirical method, we should determine what the actions are 'to which we must attribute *genuine moral worth*' (1995: 130), but these actions will not be the same when 'we' have the higher degree of compassion as when 'we' have only the lower degree.

By contrast, Sandra Shapshay interprets Schopenhauer as following the Kantian line of 'enjoining us to harm no one even if doing so would bring about better consequences all things considered' (2019: 184), apparently taking this injunction to hold for all of us, irrespective of the degree of our compassion. We have, however, quoted Schopenhauer's scathing comment on Kant's formula about the impermissibility of using humans merely as means. Shapshay appears oblivious to this fact and asserts that 'the crux of Schopenhauer's criticism' (2019: 177) of this formula is that Kant restricts the ban on the use of beings as mere means to *human* beings. In her view Schopenhauer favours an extension of this ban to all sentient beings, since things can be good and bad for all such creatures, though to a lower degree than for rational creatures (2019: 187–91).

However, this would seem to have the absurd implication that we are not allowed to harm even an insect (assuming that it is sentient) as a mere means to producing the best outcome all things considered. In addition, this proposal does not seem to square with how Schopenhauer morally justifies eating animals: 'the capacity for suffering keeps pace with intelligence, and thus man will suffer more by going without food...than the animal does through a quick and always unforeseen death' (1995: 182). If, however, I am right in thinking that he might accept that the Kantian formula be limited to those who are capable of reasonable objecting, it would not apply to (most) non-human animals.

That Schopenhauer could let the positive imperative of helping overrule the negative one of non-harming is, however, just a speculation about what he could plausibly say if pressed, not a claim about what he does say. It is something that he could say even if, as I shall argue, he must surrender his view that the lower form of compassion has to do with justice, and that justice consists in complying with the imperative 'Injure nobody'. It is more plausible to claim that a lower form or grade of compassion expresses itself in compliance with this imperative than that justice does, for doing what is just could consist in injuring someone if this is deserved, as will soon be exemplified. Also, if what expresses itself in this imperative is simply compassion of a lower grade than that which expresses itself in the imperative 'Help everyone as much as you can', it is natural that the latter takes precedence.

But if we indulge in such speculations, we leave behind what I shall concentrate on in this book: what might be called his *manifest morality*, which is constituted exclusively by moral doctrines that he *explicitly* and *unequivocally* endorses, that are 'upfront' in his works, his 'official' morality. It follows that Schopenhauer exegesis will not occupy any central place here, though I shall occasionally advance suggestions that go beyond his manifest morality, as with the 'double-standard' account that I have just offered. This will be when discussions of components of his manifest morality throw up puzzles, like what he would say when the two limbs of his conjunctive imperative conflict, as they clearly regularly will.

It is a well-known fact that spontaneous compassion is often partial in ways that many of us find unjustifiable: we feel more compassion for sufferers who are present to our senses, who are cute or familiar, who are members of our own race or species, and so on. This suffices to show that we cannot identify compassion in its raw, actual form with moral motivation. It is rather compassion *refined or rectified by proper moral reflection* that is fit to exemplify moral motivation. But deriving morality from compassion thus qualified would be patently circular, for to identify relevant instances of compassion, it has to be determined what correctly counts as 'proper moral reflection', and this presupposes a grasp of what is moral. As will emerge in 1.3 and 3.4, at its peak the compassion on which Schopenhauer bases morality requires an insight into the nature of things that is reserved for very few. It cannot be plausibly claimed that it is an empirical fact that this highly refined compassion would be universally agreed to be the basis of morality. However that may be, in Chapter 3 I shall defend the Schopenhauerian view that compassion is sensitive to reflection.

I shall, however, offer no complete account of what moral reflection is. One important reason why I shall not do this is that, like Schopenhauer, I believe moral motivation comprises a sense of justice, which I take to involve a conception of what is just or fair as well as motivation to do what is conceived to be just or fair. But, although I agree with him that compassion can serve the cause of justice by 'counteracting egoistic or malicious motives', I am convinced that our concern for justice is independent of compassion.

This is shown by the fact that it can *conflict* with compassion, for instance, when it drives us to punish somebody who is guilty of crimes (cf. Cartwright, 2012; Shapshay, 2019: 163–4). Kant's (in)famous judgement that justice requires that the last murderer be executed before a society is dissolved could exemplify a stark expression of this sentiment. But a concern for justice could not just conflict with compassion by motivating us to contravene the imperative about not injuring; it could also motivate us to contravene the imperative of helping everyone as much as we can without injuring anyone. For it could impel us to withhold help that compassion tempts us to bestow on those who are justly badly off. Or when we have to choose between helping those who are better off more or those who are worse off less, it could motivate us to help the latter because this results in a distribution that is more just, though the sum of help distributed is less. In 1.4 and 2.3 I shall develop the view that we have an intrinsic desire to do what we judge to be just or fair which is distinct from compassion and our intrinsic desire to make things go better for those who suffer.

What justice or fairness *really* consists in is a hotly debated issue which I shall not attempt to settle here. Consequently, I cannot determine what motivation is morally correct all things considered, since this would have to include at least a judicious combination of morally proper compassion and a morally proper sense of justice, consisting, for instance, in that the latter justifiably constrains excessive compassion for those who are near and dear.

1.2 Compassion and Other Moral Attitudes Based on Empathy

Compassion has a *negative* orientation: it is sympathizing with the *pain, suffering, unhappiness, sorrow*, etc. of another. Since Schopenhauer, like Buddhists, emphasizes the negative side of existence, it is not surprising that he follows them in fastening on a negatively oriented attitude such as compassion. But, surely, an attitude which 'incites me to active help', to benefit others or make them better off, need not have such a negative orientation: it could instead aim to boost their pleasure, joy, or happiness. Schopenhauer denies this, however, affirming: 'Direct sympathy with another is restricted to his *suffering*' (1995: 145). He continues:

> The reason for this is that pain, suffering that includes all want, privation, need, in fact every wish or desire, is *that which is positive and directly felt and experienced*. On the other hand, the nature of satisfaction, enjoyment, and happiness consists solely in the removal of a privation, the stilling of a pain; and so these have a *negative* effect. Therefore, need and desire are the condition of every pleasure or enjoyment. (1995: 146)

This is a view that readily leads to his claim that 'it would be better for us not to exist' which he hails as 'the most important of all truths' (1966: II, 605).

These are doubtless claims that strike many of us as highly counter-intuitive. In line with this reaction, I shall in Chapter 4 argue that positive feelings, pleasure, enjoyment, happiness and so on are feelings in their own right, and not just the disappearance of the negative feelings of pain, suffering, unhappiness etc. The existence of positive feelings makes it more appropriate to speak of *sympathy* than compassion. For, as Adam Smith pointed out, in contrast to 'pity' and 'compassion', 'the emotion which we feel for the misery of others', 'sympathy' may 'without much impropriety, be made use of to denote our fellow-feeling with any passion whatever' (1790: I.i.1.5).[4] In the interest of clarity, I shall sometimes tack 'positive' or 'negative' onto 'sympathy', and use 'sympathetic joy' as a positive counterpart to compassion. The terms 'compassion' and 'pity' could be taken as rough synonymous, but I shall avoid 'pity' because it has a pejorative ring that 'compassion' lacks, for example, when we speak of wallowing in self-pity, or in heated arguments condescendingly exclaim that we pity our adversaries (cf. Cartwright, 1988: 559–60).

Sympathy should be distinguished from *empathy*. Empathizing with someone is, I maintain, *imagining* feeling how you believe this individual to be feeling rather than actually feeling this. (In 3.1 I shall add that these feelings must be *good or bad* for the subject.) As this implies, such a piece of imagination involves a belief about how the individual in question is feeling. But imagining the occurrence of something is different from believing or thinking that it is occurring;

---

[4] According to Schopenhauer's idiosyncratic definition of 'Sympathie' (1966: II, 601–2), which I shall ignore, it covers compassion, but also e.g. love. It is defined as 'the empirical appearance of the will's metaphysical identity, through the physical multiplicity of its phenomena'.

if you imagine seeing a kea, it is unlikely that you believe or think that you are seeing one. Imagining seeing a kea is having an experience that is *qualitatively like* seeing a kea, but usually less vivid. So imagining feeling e.g. pain usually affects you less than actually feeling pain, though it may well cause you some discomfort.

You normally succeed in imagining seeing a kea because you have a correct belief about what it is (like) to have an experience of seeing a kea, a belief that for the most part is derived from a memory of having had the experience of seeing one. Imagining seeing a kea is something that you can probably do voluntarily if you have seen one fairly recently, but it is also something that it is likely to happen to you non-voluntarily—and even involuntarily—e.g. if somebody starts talking about New Zealand parrots in these circumstances.

Imagining how you believe another is feeling should not be conflated with imagining how you believe that *you* would be feeling were you in that individual's circumstances.[5] This may be what, e.g. Adam Smith has in mind:

> By the imagination we place ourselves in his situation, we conceive ourselves enduring all the same torments, we enter as it were into his body and become in some measure the same person with him, and thence form some idea of his sensations, and even feel something which, though weaker in degree, is not altogether unlike them. (1790: I.i.1.2)

How you believe that you would be feeling were you in someone else's circumstances could, however, be quite different from how you believe that individual is feeling if you are psychologically radically different than this individual.

It might be retorted that there is no difference if you imagine yourself to resemble the other individual in relevant respects. This might be what Smith means with 'we enter as it were into his body and become in some measure the same person with him', since later he writes more explicitly that we should 'not only change circumstances' with this individual, but 'persons and characters' as well (1790: VII. iii.1.4). To be sure, the more you imagine shedding your own features and acquiring the features of somebody else, the more what you

---

[5] Cf. Amy Coplan's distinction between self-oriented and other-oriented perspective-taking (2011: 9–15).

imagine that you believe that you would be feeling would be like what you believe that this individual would be feeling. But it is only if you imagine being *exactly* like this individual in every relevant respect that these two things will coincide, and then there is unlikely to be enough left of you for it to make sense to say that it is *yourself* that you imagine being in the other individual's situation: are you not just imagining *someone* like that individual having the feelings in question? Contrariwise, the greater the extent to which you fail to rid the being imagined of relevant features of yourself, the less good you are at empathizing with this individual.

Smith notes, in accordance with what was mentioned above: 'It is the impressions of our own senses only... which our imaginations copy' (1790: I.i.1.2). But it does not follow from this observation that when we (try to) empathize with somebody else, we imagine feeling as we believe that we ourselves would be feeling were we in this individual's place. What we imagine feeling could still be what we believe that the other individual is feeling, for we may take it for granted that what this individual is feeling is the same as what we would be feeling. Colour-blindness was not scientifically described until 1794, by John Dalton. Hitherto, it had apparently been generally assumed that people experience colours in the same ways, and that other humans have the same sense-impressions in the same external circumstances as we do is still something that we spontaneously assume.

If what individuals feel in the same type of situations often differs, and what we imagine feeling when we imagine feeling what we believe another is feeling is modelled on our own feelings, it may be wondered, first, how close the match between the feelings that we imagine and the actual feelings of the other is likely to be and, secondly, whether it is close enough for our imagining to qualify as empathy. As regards the first question, we can tell at least that the match can be close enough for the emotional reaction to the feelings imagined to count as sympathizing with what the other is feeling. In reply to the second question, it must be admitted that the concept of empathy is too vague for the question of how close the match must be for there to be empathy to have a definite answer; all we can say is presumably, in Smith's words, that empathy requires that the feelings imagined must not be 'altogether unlike' the feelings of the target. We might, however, partly accommodate this problem of vagueness by distinguishing between higher and lower grades of empathy. I shall return to this problem in 3.1, but without coming up with a satisfactory solution.

But even if imagining how you believe that you would be feeling in someone else's circumstances will not do as an explication of what it is to empathize with this individual, imagining yourself in something like someone else's circumstances—external or internal—could still play a moral role. If you are cold-hearted towards somebody who unawares happens to be in a miserable situation—e.g. by being exposed to an external or internal threat—through bad luck and no fault of their own, imaginatively representing yourself being in this situation might well make you concerned to alleviate the badness of this situation, since the fact that you are normally concerned about yourself will rub off. It might also alert you to the possibility that you yourself could end up in a similar situation and, thereby, be inclined to make its occurrence less probable. But if, as is likely, you then feel sorry for the individual in the miserable situation, this is not feeling compassion for the individual by means of empathizing, since you are not imagining what you believe this individual to be feeling. For your imagination is chiefly exploiting your knowledge of circumstances of which this individual is not conscious.

There are, then, morally relevant features of our circumstances that are not a matter of our feelings or experiences. This can be illustrated by the moral badness of being victims of injustice, who are not aware of the injustice because they are not aware of the fact that they are worse off than others, or that this is unjust because it is due to bad luck and no fault of their own. To imagine lively what it would be like to be such an individual, being a victim of injustice without being conscious of it, could be an effective means of making yourself feel sorry for these individuals and increase your motivation to rectify the injustice that afflicts them. But, to repeat, this is not empathy and compassion.

Likewise, the fact that people whom we assume to be our friends deceive us so cunningly that we never discover their deceitfulness is reasonably something that detracts from the value of our lives, though it is not anything that we experience or feel.[6] Imagining people being

---

[6] For further discussion of this point, see Persson (2017: ch.1.2). In (2017: pt. II), I also argue that the value of justice is impersonal as opposed to personal.

thus deceived is therefore something that could make us feel sorry for them, though this emotion does not qualify as sympathy or compassion, since it is not based on imagining feelings that they are believed to experience.

As noted, when we imagine feeling something, we ultimately have to draw on instances of ourselves having had the feeling, but when we are aware that the individual whose situation we imagine does not have the feeling, we cannot ascribe the feeling imagined to this individual. What is essential then is that our feeling of being subject to injustice or whatever is one that it is *correct* to have rather than that the victim shares it. By contrast, when you are in the business of empathizing and dealing with experiential aspects of another's situation, it is whether the victim has something like the relevant experience that is decisive. Still, it should not be forgotten that there are non-experiential, morally relevant features that empathy cannot reach and, thus, that for moral purposes our imagination has to cast its net wider.

In the sense of interest here, sympathy involves empathy, but in addition it involves in the case of compassion feeling sad because of the suffering (sadness, etc.) that you imagine another is feeling. Furthermore, it normally involves having a benevolent desire to alleviate this suffering as an end in itself, that is, just in order to make this individual feel better—if you believe that you can do something to achieve this end. But it is not necessary that you have such a belief: you may feel compassion for the suffering of somebody who, say, is caught in a burning building, though you are dead certain that you cannot do anything to relieve their suffering.[7]

---

[7] Martha Nussbaum's conception of compassion is that 'some combination of imaginative reconstruction with the judgment that the person is in distress and that this distress is bad' 'comes close to being compassion'. The reason that she gives for why it might not be the same is the possibility of 'compassion without imaginative reconstruction [of someone's experiences]' (2001: 305), i.e. without empathy. This conception of compassion is importantly different from mine, apart from Nussbaum's reservation about its inclusion of empathy. First, true to her general view of emotions, it equates compassion with judgements. I have argued against this view elsewhere (2005: 63–4), where I also expound my own view of what emotions are (chs. 5 & 6). Briefly and bluntly, I cannot see how the view that emotions *are* judgements can do justice to the obvious point that emotions are something we *feel*, sometimes quite violently. Secondly, although I think that the object of compassion for somebody consists in something that is bad *for* them, like suffering—this seems

The counterpart emotion of positive sympathy is feeling glad because of the enjoyment (happiness, etc.) that you imagine another is feeling, along with standardly having a benevolent desire to prolong this enjoyment if you think that you can do something to this effect. Again, it is not necessary that you think that this is something in your power.

Confusingly, there is, however, a sense of 'sympathy' in which it does not involve empathy. This is the sense in which sympathizing with the attitude of another means being in agreement with or sharing this attitude, the sense that we would have in mind were we to say, for instance, that we sympathize with somebody's dislike of a political party when we dislike it as they do. It is the sense that Smith appears to be employing when he writes: 'To approve of the passions of another... as suitable to their objects, is the same thing as to observe that we entirely sympathize with them' (1790: I.i.3.1). Sympathizing here is unlikely to involve our imagining feeling the dislike that we believe others to be feeling, and although our dislike could well motivate us to actions against the party in question that would satisfy their dislike, we are probably not motivated to perform those actions with the end of satisfying their dislike. It is important that we do not let the existence of this kind of sympathy lead us astray.

It might be suggested that it is in accordance with everyday use to restrict terms like 'empathy' and 'empathize' to situations in which we imagine feeling something that we (more or less) correctly believe an actual individual is actually feeling at the moment, and 'compassion' and 'sympathetic joy' to the emotions of sadness or gladness that this imagining induces. But, although this situation may be what we are most familiar with, we should not think that it is all. For instance, it seems that we could empathize with what somebody, now deceased, felt when they first heard that they had been diagnosed with a terminal illness, and feel compassion for them. Whatever the limits of its everyday use, we should concede that there is something relevantly like empathy and empathizing even in situations in which we imagine

---

to me to be a conceptual truth—I doubt that it involves a judgement that this is bad full stop or absolutely. I am inclined to understand this as meaning *morally* bad, but I think that you could feel compassion for somebody who is close to you whilst being conscious that this feeling is morally unjustified, say, because you are convinced that their suffering is deserved and, thus, not morally bad.

the feelings that we believe an actual individual would be feeling in an entirely imaginary situation, or that we believe an imaginary or fictive individual would be feeling, and that the generated emotions of being sorry or glad for these individuals' sake are analogous to compassion and sympathetic joy. It is convenient to widen the terms 'empathy', 'compassion', and 'sympathy' to cover these circumstances if they do not do so in ordinary parlance.

Since, as regards morality, our interest is primarily in what motivates (intentional) *action*, it is *benevolence* that we should focus on. As will be seen in more detail in Chapter 3, benevolence can occur in the absence of sympathy, so its scope is broader in this respect. For instance, the thought of the good life that an individual who could develop out of an embryo is likely to have could elicit benevolence from us—especially if we imagine this life in some detail—which motivates us to keep the embryo alive, though we cannot sympathize with the embryo. For while the object of sympathetic joy and compassion has to be an actual or imaginary sentient being, the object of the sort of desire that as a rule is their companion could be that such a being with positive feelings begins to exist, or that such a being with negative feelings does not begin to exist. On the other hand, compassion can be felt where there is no space for benevolence, e.g. for the deceased individual just mentioned.

An important aspect of desires is that they can be modified in a fashion that the bodily reactions that are felt in emotions cannot. Desires can be channelled into action plans that can be intentionally executed, and this could result in them having objects that sympathy cannot have. For example, we cannot feel sympathy for each and every member of a large crowd of sufferers, but we can sympathize with a single sufferer representing them, understand intellectually how much bigger the total suffering of the crowd must be, and channel the resulting benevolence into an action strategy that is designed to benefit the entire crowd. Our benevolence could thus be said to be oriented at the entire crowd, though we may have to sacrifice so much more to implement such a strategy effectively than a strategy directed at fewer sufferers that we shall fail to do so.[8]

---

[8] As I argue in (2005: 72–3), emotions are passive states because their objects have to do with what evokes them, whereas desires are active states because their

Let us say that we are *concerned* about how someone feels if we are *disposed* to have in suitable circumstances a benevolent desire for its own sake that they will feel well rather than badly. We shall then also be disposed to feel sympathy with positive feelings that we think they might have, and compassion on account of their negative feelings, unless we are able to help them extinguish their feelings so quickly that we do not have time to feel anything of this sort.

We should therefore bear in mind that sympathy, in a positive or negative form, and benevolent or altruist desires are distinct attitudes that could occur in the absence of each other. But I shall generally assume that these desires are present when the emotion of sympathy broadly conceived is present. Strictly speaking, however, it is benevolence rather than sympathy which is the moral motivator. As will be explained in 3.2, we can acquire habits of acting on the basis of benevolent desires which enable us to take action before we have time to feel sympathy.

Additionally, it should be noted that there is a form of concern which is not concern about something's well-being or welfare and which does not involve empathy. We can have such concern for sentient beings in our childhood, before having developed the capacity for empathy, and for inanimate objects throughout our lives. It is a disposition that manifests itself in desires to protect its objects, e.g. works of art, against destruction and damage, and in fear that they might be destroyed or damaged if we believe them to be exposed to threats that we cannot avert. Since inanimate objects cannot be benefited or harmed, desires to treat them well cannot be characterized as benevolence, and desires to treat them badly are not malevolence.

It is possible to empathize with someone without sympathizing with them—indeed, you might even feel *schadenfreude* because of their suffering or misery. This happens when imagining someone's plight makes you glad rather than sad. The fact that *schadenfreude* involves empathy could be brought out by situations in which it is transformed into compassion. If you hear that somebody who has taken pleasure in your suffering a misfortune suffers a misfortune

---

objects have to do with what they are designed to bring about. My most elaborate account of intentional action is expounded in (2019).

roughly in the same measure as you did, you might feel *schadenfreude*. But if you are later told that their suffering is in fact much greater, amounting to hellish agony, your *schadenfreude* might well be replaced by compassion. This could not have happened if you had not been imagining with some degree of vividness what their suffering was like.

It may seem odd to hold that *schadenfreude* could involve empathy, but that is probably because 'empathy' is sometimes used as a synonym of 'sympathy', or that sympathy is assumed always to accompany empathy and *schadenfreude* never does.[9] It is also odd to say that you empathize if you are callous or cold-hearted in the sense that imagining the suffering of others leaves you emotionally indifferent, but this is likely because empathy to a notable degree seldom leaves people indifferent. When people are callous or cold-hearted, this is probably most frequently due to a lack of empathy and, as a result, sympathy.

Stephen Darwall adopts a view similar to mine: 'Empathy can be consistent with the indifference of pure observation or even the cruelty of sadism' (1998: 261). In this context, he comments: 'if one is inclined to believe that another's feelings are not warranted by her situation, this will make it more difficult to share them through projective empathy' (1998: 269).[10] Since most of us do not regard the joy or enjoyment of sadists as warranted by the suffering they inflict, we do not spontaneously empathize with them, and since this is so, we are probably prone to think that they cannot spontaneously empathize with their victims.

---

[9] Frans de Waal is ambivalent. On the one hand, he writes: 'Having been duped by someone, we show the opposite of empathy. At our seeing his pain, the brain's *pleasure* centers light up... Such Schadenfreude occurs only in men, however' (2010: 72). The claim that empathy is 'the opposite' of *schadenfreude* seems to make sense only if empathy is taken to be or imply sympathy. Yet he denies this elsewhere: 'Empathy is the process by which we gather information about someone else. Sympathy, in contrast, reflects concern about the other' (2010: 88). The explanation of such a vacillation is, I surmise, that empathy does not *entail* sympathy, but is as a rule accompanied by it. By the way, it is interesting if *schadenfreude* is more common in men (and compassion in women).

[10] Darwall takes emotional contagion to be the 'most rudimentary form of empathy' (1998: 264). As will be discussed in 3.1, I find emotional contagion so different from what I label 'empathy' that it would be misleading to employ the same term for both. Darwall's 'projective empathy' corresponds to 'empathy' in my terminology.

But Darwall makes a mistake when in connection with this comment he claims that when we empathize 'we place ourselves in the other's situation and try to work out what *to* feel' (1998: 268). Working out what to feel in a certain situation, or what *should* be felt in it (cf. 1998: 261), and imagining feeling it, is not empathizing with the individual in that situation if he or she is not believed to feel anything like it. It is one thing to maintain that we do not in general empathize with feelings that we believe to be unwarranted or improper; it is another thing to maintain that when we imagine having feelings that are warranted or proper, our attitude is one of empathy. If, in spite of the fact that we consider them unwarranted, we were to imagine having feelings that we correctly believe somebody to have, we would be empathizing with them.

1.3 Moral versus Anti-Moral Attitudes

Although I differ from Schopenhauer in viewing positive feelings of pleasure and the like to be feelings in their own right as much as negative feelings, I shall contend in Chapter 4 that there is *an asymmetry or bias in favour of the negative* to the effect that the badness for the subject of negative feelings and their underlying conditions is usually of a greater magnitude than the goodness for the subject of positive feelings and their underlying conditions. This leads to compassion with subjects who fare badly often being justifiably stronger or more intense than our sympathetic joy with those who fare well. Likewise, benevolence is likely to be justifiably stronger when its objective is to reduce negative feelings than to produce positive feelings. This might also hold, *mutatis mutandis*, for malevolence: it might be stronger when its objective is to produce negative feelings than to reduce equal positive feelings. And *schadenfreude* might be more intense if the former than if the latter happens.

There is a related matter on which my view differs from Schopenhauer's. His characterization of our motive of *malice* or *malevolence* is that it 'makes its ultimate aim the *pain* of another' (1995: 145). By contrast, when the suffering of another evokes my compassion and benevolence, he asserts that I must in some sense feel the suffering as *my own*: I must '*feel it with him, feel it as my own*, and yet not *within me*, but *in another person*' (1995: 165). When the suffering of another evokes malevolence, I do not 'feel it as my own', but simply as the suffering of another individual. Thus, compassion (alongside benevolence) with someone necessitates that 'I am in some way *identified with him*, in other words, that this entire *difference* between me and everyone else, which is the very basis of my egoism, is eliminated... the non-ego has to a certain extent become the ego' (1995: 143–4). In other words, we seem to have something like an expansion of the ego so that it includes the individual for whom I am feeling compassion. It is something like an *extended egoism* that makes this attitude possible.

Schopenhauer's view, then, appears to be that, whereas representing another as suffering could by itself motivate us to prolong or intensify this suffering—proving us to be malicious or malevolent—it could not by itself motivate us to mitigate it. Such benevolence requires in addition that in some way we feel the other's suffering 'as our own'. As opposed to this, I shall in 2.2 argue that a representation of suffering by itself, whether it be the suffering of oneself or another, could motivate compassion and benevolence, since personal identity does not matter, as Derek Parfit has argued.

It may be asked how I could feel suffering both 'as my own' and yet 'in another person'. As will be suggested in 2.4, Schopenhauer's reply could appeal to his distinction between the world as it is given in experience, in the dimensions of space and time, and the world as a thing-in-itself, outside the '*principium individuationis*' of space and time:

> Individuation is mere phenomenon or appearance and originates through space and time. These are nothing but the forms of all of the objects of my cerebral cognitive faculty and are conditioned by them. And so even the plurality and diversity of individuals are mere phenomenon, that is, exist only in *my representation*. My true inner being exists in every living thing as directly as it makes itself known in my self-consciousness only to me. (1995: 210)

Schopenhauer could claim that, although compassionate people realize that spatio-temporal individuation is an illusion that effaces a real identity and oneness behind, it does not make them entirely oblivious to this individuation. Hence, the double-sided character of compassionate people's attitude to others. My own account of sympathy involves something that I believe to be metaphysically less extravagant than a denial of distinctness, namely, a denial of the importance attaching to our identity, as mentioned. If our being motivated to relieve our own suffering is independent of our imaginatively representing it as our own, it is not mysterious how our imaginatively representing the suffering of others could motivate us equally to relieve it.[11]

According to Schopenhauer's view, then, compassion is underpinned by a more complex representational content—one that comprises an extra element of identification with another—than malevolence or malice. On my view, it is rather the other way around: the mechanism of compassion and benevolence is simpler, for whilst being malevolent towards somebody requires that we dislike this individual *for some (perhaps quite feeble) reason*, compassion or benevolence towards another does not require liking this individual in particular. Liking somebody for some reason rather *enhances* sympathy or benevolence that could be present in the absence of the reason. You could sympathize with a total stranger who is suffering before your eyes, but you would not have a malevolent desire that the suffering of another be prolonged, unless you dislike this individual for some reason. We are normally so wired up that vividly imagining what it is like for somebody to suffer by itself, without considering the particulars of this individual, elicits compassion and benevolence if it elicits any emotional or conative reaction. When *schadenfreude* and malevolence instead are elicited, it is in fact because of the influence of some disliked property that the sufferer is thought to possess.

It makes evolutionary sense that a kind of being who is regularly dependent on help from its fellows is equipped with a disposition to empathize and sympathize with them straight off when they are observed to be screaming, writhing etc. But it also makes evolutionary sense to hypothesize that many of the beings confronted have properties that prevent empathy from being generated and, consequently, leave others indifferent or cold-hearted, for otherwise their helpfulness is liable to be overworked and exploited. These are not always

---

[11] David Cartwright also offers a re-interpretation that drops the metaphysical element and instead takes compassion to involve that someone 'participates imaginatively' in the suffering of another (2008: 303). In 2.4 Shapshay's 'axiological' attempt to drop this element will also be critically examined.

properties that provide reasons for negative attitudes like *schadenfreude* and malevolence; this would result in hostile responses instead being overworked. There are such properties that so to speak notch up indifference to antipathy, but they are rather counterparts to properties that notch up positive attitudes of sympathy from lower to higher levels.

The reason for which we can maliciously desire that some misfortune afflicts another could not be any reason, however. We cannot desire this as a means to the satisfaction of a *self-interested* desire. For example, if I wish you to get injured so that you cannot win a contest, my attitude to you might be one of malice and, if I am glad upon hearing that you have indeed been injured, I might be feeling *schadenfreude*. But this is so only if my desire that you do not win the contest is not motivated by a self-interested desire of mine, such as that my own chance of winning the contest will thereby improve. Malice cannot be motivated by self-interest; in this respect, it is like benevolence and compassion, as Schopenhauer points out (1995: 145).

All the same, I would not be harbouring malice towards you unless there was something about you that makes me dislike you, and this may well have to do with your having thwarted my self-interested desires in the past. This could provide me with a reason to want that you will be unable to compete successfully, but if my attitude is to be one of malice, it cannot be that I see your failure to be a serious contender merely as a means of improving my own prospects. For its being such a means is compatible with it being something that I *regret* having to rely on, and this is at odds with my maliciously wanting you to be injured. If I am malicious, I must want you to fail at least partly because it is *bad for you*, because it will thwart your self-interested desires, not only because it will be good for me or some else. What is bad for another is an *end in itself* for the malevolent person. Likewise, when my attitude towards you is benevolence, I must want things for you because they are good for you; what is good for you must be an end of mine. But benevolence and malevolence differ in that, whilst we do not harbour malevolence unless we dislike its target for some reason, we could harbour benevolence, even though we do not like its target in particular, though our benevolence will then naturally be weaker.

Moreover, in order to exhibit malice and *schadenfreude*, it must also be the case that I do not desire your failure and feel pleasure upon learning that it hits you because I think that it is *just or fair* that you fail, or justified by promoting some moral end, such as letting somebody who more badly needs to win to be victorious. But I must not think that it is unjust or unjustified that you fail, either. Our malice and *schadenfreude* must occur independently of our considering the issue of the justice or moral justification of the harm afflicting its target.

When we feel pleased about someone's being harmed independently of considering whether or not they deserve it, or it is justified, it is usually the case that the harm is suffered by somebody who is disliked by us because they have somehow harmed or negatively affected ourselves or somebody or something, e.g. our nation, with which we identify. Then we are liable to be carried away by a disproportionally strong desire that the perpetrator be harmed in return, without stopping to consider whether or not the magnitude of the harm that we want inflicted would be deserved or justified. For the most part, the magnitude will then be greater than would be deserved and justified, since we are partial in our own favour. Still, we feel pleased or satisfied—that is, feel *schadenfreude*—when we learn that harm whose absolute magnitude matches what we crave is inflicted on the perpetrator, though it is likely to be greater than is in fact deserved and justified. This explains why malice and *schadenfreude* are immoral: it is a matter of desiring that others suffer more than is in fact deserved or justified, and being pleased when they are thought to suffer thus.[12]

---

[12] Contrary to what I have proposed, Richard Smith in a book on *schadenfreude* uses a 'broad definition' of it (2013: xiii), according to which it 'arises because there are varied ways that we can gain from other people's misfortunes' (2013: xviii). This permits *schadenfreude* to consist in the satisfaction of self-interest. Also, although he notes that pleasure due to another's deserved misfortune 'may seem qualitatively different from *schadenfreude*' (2013: 204, n. 4), he still counts this pleasure as *schadenfreude*. There is no name for pleasure or satisfaction because someone is thought to suffer as much as they deserve. The term 'satisfied indignation' has been proposed (Kristjánsson, 2005: 60), but it strikes me as something of a contradiction in terms, since indignation seems to consist in *dis*satisfaction and anger because someone gets more of the good or bad than they deserve. I think, however, that we should not expect there to be such a term because what satisfaction we feel when we learn that someone suffers a misfortune that we think that they deserve varies a lot depending on whether our sympathies lie with this individual, the victims harmed, or nowhere. Additionally, the satisfaction that we feel when we hear that someone

For Schopenhauer *schadenfreude* is even the most 'infallible sign of a thoroughly bad heart and profound moral worthlessness' (1995: 135).

1.4 Justice-Based Attitudes

I agree with Schopenhauer that our concern for our own well-being is not *moral* concern; only concern for the well-being of others could be moral concern. But why is that if, as I am going to contend, we are not concerned about our own well-being because it is our own? Chapter 2 provides the answer. It will be seen that the answer cannot have to do with the well-being being our own, since our concern for the well-being of some individuals who are numerically distinct from us resembles self-concern in not being classifiable as moral. Instead, it has to do with their being distinct from ourselves in ways that provide our empathy with another type of basis and that make possible relations of justice to them.

As already remarked, Schopenhauer would have done better had he claimed that moral motivation consists in (positive or negative) sympathy rather than compassion, but he would still be vulnerable to the objection that the motivational source of morality also comprises our sense of or concern for justice, and this is a source that is independent of sympathy. Our sense of justice is not just a motive that prevents us from harming others, as he presents it. It can express itself in this way, but it can also express itself in harmful behaviour, for example, when we harm somebody whom we believe deserves to be harmed, e.g. by punishing someone whom we believe to have caused harm knowingly. In the context of justice, compassion (along with benevolence) could assume the shape of *mercy* or *clemency* by not letting somebody suffer as much as they deserve. But compassion could also join forces with justice, for instance, when we adopt it towards those who suffer unjustly and, thus, become more willing to benefit them and harm to an extent that is just those who make them suffer.

The punishment of wrong-doers often expresses *anger* (or indignation) at them. The emotion of anger is bound up with the concept of

---

receives something bad that they deserve may be the same as when they receive something good that they deserve, especially if the individuals involved are neither liked nor disliked by us.

desert: when we are angry at somebody, we see them as deserving to be punished and blamed because they have harmed ourselves or others. On the other hand, when we feel *gratitude* towards somebody, we take it that they deserve a good return and praise for having benefited us or others. Anger and gratitude belong to a set of responses that frequently goes by the name of *tit-for-tat*.

Other emotions belonging to the set of desert-involving emotions include, to give a rough-and-ready characterization of them (for more detail, see Persson, 2005: ch. 6): feeling *guilty* which is feeling that we deserve blame or punishment because we have acted wrongly in some way; feeling *ashamed* or, about less serious matters, *embarrassed*, that is, feeling that we are blameworthy because we fall short of some standard of behaviour, and *proud* when we take ourselves to be praiseworthy because we surpass some standard of behaviour; feeling *forgiveness* which involves withdrawing our earlier opinion that others deserve blame and punishment for their wrongful behaviour, perhaps because they have shown *remorse*—which comprises these people wishing that they had acted otherwise than they did—or we realize that they were not responsible for their wrongful behaviour. *Admiration* and *contempt* are counterparts to pride and shame when the targets are people with whom we cannot identify in a sense in which we can identify with others with whom we are closely associated, such as our family or even compatriots.

It is plausible to think that if dispositions to feel these emotions are widespread in a population, this population tends to do better than populations in which these motivational traits are rare or non-existent. Take gratitude and anger: if one individual who has been groomed gratefully returns this service, this mutually beneficial cooperation is likely to continue, with the result that the probability of the cooperators being infested by parasites decreases. On the other hand, if some individuals do not return favours, it is useful to react with anger or indignation and punish them by excluding them from exploitation of the helpfulness of others. Mutually advantageous cooperation is likely to continue if directed at those who reciprocate but excludes free-riders. Pride and shame can be useful because they encourage people to continue to behave in beneficial ways and discourage them from harmful behaviour, respectively. The same goes for admiration and contempt.

Desert is a concept of justice (or fairness): if you deserve some treatment then, other things being equal, it is just that you receive it.

It follows that individuals who are equipped with desert-involving responses have some sense of justice. But then we land in a view which contradicts that of David Hume, who famously taught that justice is an 'artifice', i.e. something that 'is not deriv'd from nature, but arises artificially, tho' necessarily from education, and human conventions' (1739–40: 483). The conception of justice is a pre-cultural conception, traces of which can be found in some of the more social and intelligent species of our mammalian ancestors (e.g. capuchin monkeys, as demonstrated by de Waal, 2010: 187–8), and which children acquire very early in their development.

Another concept of justice is the *rights* ascribed to individuals for, in the absence of other relevant factors, it is unjust to rob someone of something to which they have a right, even if someone else needs it more.[13] The notion of a right, too, can plausibly be traced to behavioural dispositions exhibited by our animal predecessors, specifically to the special ferocity with which they defend their offspring, turf, or food. This ferocity provides a reason for others to leave these things alone—a reason expressed by the notion of a right. The 'other side' of these rights is corresponding negative *duties* or *obligations* of others not to interfere with us and our property.

Commonsensical thinking about justice is largely conducted in terms of deserts and rights, but even if these concepts are regarded as inapplicable to us, it need not be denied, as is done by utilitarians, that justice has an important role to play in morality. For an *egalitarian* conception of justice may be defended, as it has been by myself (e.g. in 2017: ch. 7). I believe that there is a principle of justice which requires everyone to be equally well off, unless there is something—such as deserts and rights—that makes it just that some are worse off than others, or some autonomously choose to be worse off. Then, if there is nothing to make it just that some are worse off than others, justice requires everyone to be equally well off, unless some autonomously choose to be worse off.

---

[13] If another needs the right-covered item a lot more, this may make depriving the right-holder of this item *morally justified* in terms of reasons of beneficence. As indicated, being just is not the only way of being morally justified: being justified in terms of beneficence is another.

In this work, however, I shall not defend any particular conception of justice. My point is merely that, whatever we take justice to consist in, it is for us a source of moral motivation that is independent of (positive or negative) sympathy and benevolence. Even if both benevolence and our concern for justice motivate us to benefit individuals whom we take to suffer unjustly, there is a difference between them: benevolence motivates us to benefit them *for their own good*, just to make them better off, while our sense of justice motivates us to benefit these individuals *to the extent required by justice*. The latter might well motivate us to benefit these individuals to a lesser extent than the former, e.g. if the individuals who unjustly suffer are near and dear to us, spontaneous benevolence may induce us to benefit them more than justice allows.

There are factors that facilitate as well hinder our sympathy and benevolence. Facilitating factors include: an appearance or psychological properties that are attractive or similar to our own, and simply being present to our senses as opposed to being known merely by some sketchy description. But even if perceptually present, others may be out of reach of our sympathy because they drown in a big crowd. Other hindering factors are if they are physically conspicuously dissimilar from us, to the extent that many non-human animals are, or just to the extent of humans of other races. These are features that tend to block empathy and sympathy, or make them more difficult and, as a consequence, tend to make us indifferent or callous to the suffering of others.

Some other features are prone to make us positively dislike others and to cause them suffering. While we do not want to harm others simply because they are outside the scope of our senses, we are likely to be hostile and malicious to individuals who are hostile to us, psychologically or physically repellent, obscene, ugly, noisy, or smelly. Individuals may—often unreasonably—be held responsible for having many of the latter features, and if that is so, they may constitute grounds for thinking them deserving harmful treatment. These factors will be canvassed especially in 2.2.

1.5 The Aim of This Book

I have presented Schopenhauer's view of compassion as the basis of morality. I have also outlined why I doubt the truth of a number of the claims that he advances in the process of expounding this view. The over-arching aim of this book is to find out with what these claims should be replaced when they have been shown to be false, or when a claim of his can be salvaged, to show how it should be revised. Summarily, I take his view of compassion as the basis of morality to consist of the following claims which he explicitly and unequivocally makes:

(1) 'Only insofar as an action has sprung from compassion does it have moral value' (1995: 144). The reason for this claim is that when acting out of compassion 'the ultimate motive for doing or omitting to do a thing is precisely and exclusively centered in the *weal or woe of someone else*' (1995: 143). In the event the ultimate object of the motive is the agent's *own* weal and woe, the motive is '*egoistic*, and consequently *without moral worth*' (1995: 143). If the ultimate end is the woe of another, as in the case of malice, it is diametrically the opposite to a moral motive.

(2) When an action has moral worth because its motive is compassion, the weal and woe of the other 'must be *directly my motive*, just as *my* weal and woe are' (1995: 143) when I am egoistically motivated. 'As soon as... compassion is aroused, the weal and woe of another are nearest to my heart in exactly the same way... as otherwise only my own are' (1995: 144). Schopenhauer takes this to be possible because we can come to realize that the spatio-temporal separation between ourselves and others is illusory and that in reality we are identical as objectification of the same will. This amounts to construing compassion as a kind of extended egoism in the sense that 'the non-ego has to a certain extent become the ego' (1995: 144).

(3) 'It is simply and solely this compassion that is the real basis of *voluntary* justice and *genuine* loving-kindness' (1995: 144); these attitudes 'are two clearly separate degrees wherein another's suffering can directly become my motive' (1995: 148). Justice is negative, less demanding and comes to expression in the imperative 'Injure no one'; loving kindness is positive, more demanding and comes to expression in the imperative 'Help everyone as much as you can'.

(4) Compassion can be impartial or unbiased, enveloping all others equally and not favouring those close to oneself. '[I]f seeing through the *principium individuationis*, if this direct knowledge of the identity of the will in all its phenomena, is present in a high degree of

distinctness' (1966: I, 378) in a person, he will 'regard the sufferings of all that lives as his own, and thus take upon himself the pain of the whole world' (1966: I, 379). But this insight is so hard to come by that very few acquire it (1966: I, 384), and it 'is not to be forcibly arrived at by intention or design, but comes...suddenly, as if flying in from without' (1966: I, 404).

(5) Compassion in its stronger loving-kindness form is a motive to help others by removing their pain and suffering. It cannot consist in producing positive feelings because there are no such: 'the nature of satisfaction, enjoyment, and happiness consists solely in the removal of a privation, the stilling of a pain' (1995: 146).

(1)–(5) are all claims that are explicitly and unambiguously stated in his discussion of morality; thus, they belong to his *manifest* morality, his official moral position. For instance, it is indisputable that Schopenhauer's explanation of compassion involves seeing through the *principium individuationis* of space and time to the identity of all and everyone in the reality behind. In 2.4 it will be seen that this explanation gives rise to several problems having to do with all of us in reality being objectifications of the same will. The thesis that positive feelings do not exist in their own right is repeated over and over in his production, albeit there are also passages in which it sounds as though he goes back on this official view of positive feelings (see e.g. Shapshay, 2019: 77). I shall put such passages aside as mere slips since, as far as I know, he never states *explicitly* that such feelings as pleasures are feelings in their own right and not just the disappearance of negative feelings.

I shall argue that nothing can salvage the truth of Schopenhauer's manifest morality, as codified by (1)–(5). My proposed replacement for (1)–(5) can be summarized thus:

(1*) Compassion is indeed an emotion whose object is the weal and woe of another for its own sake, but it is not the *only* attitude of this kind, as has been explained in the present chapter. There is also a positive counterpart of compassion: sympathetic joy, that is, joy because of the positive feelings of another, whereas compassion is sadness because of the negative feelings of another. These emotions are based on empathy, that is, *imagining* having the positive or negative feelings that one (fairly accurately) believes another to have, not actually having these feelings of the other. But empathy needs to be conceived more broadly than it ordinarily may be to cover imagining feelings that are not believed to be actual, since the emotions of sadness or gladness that this generates could be morally relevant. Additionally, and of greater moral importance, there is benevolence, i.e. a desire that another be better off as an end in itself, which often accompanies sympathy.

(2*) Positive or negative sympathy or benevolence towards another does not involve regarding the other as identical to oneself. It will be seen in 2.2 that self-concern is not grounded in taking someone as identical to oneself. Therefore, equally strong concern could in principle extend to another without this individual being seen as in some way identical to oneself. On Schopenhauer's—sound—view that egoism is not a moral attitude, his construal of compassion as requiring that 'the non-ego has to a certain extent become the ego' jeopardizes—though it might not completely undermine—the moral status of compassion and related attitudes such as sympathetic joy and benevolence. It will be argued, though, that our concern for a certain kind of individuals who are distinct from ourselves does not belong to the domain of morality.

(3*) The sense of justice can conflict with compassion and other empathy-based attitudes, including an aversion to harming, and, thus, cannot be generated by them. The sense of justice is an essential moral motive that is independent of these attitudes and in contrast to them it can motivate us to harm others. This is a more fundamental reason why compassion is not our *only* moral motive, 'the true incentive underlying *all* actions of genuine moral worth' (1995: 140, my italics) than that compassion needs to be supplemented by other empathy-based attitudes as stated in (1*). It is also argued in 2.3 that justice is restricted to those who are distinct from oneself in a way that has to do with *the independence of their will*. Herein lies the reason why justice is essentially a moral relation and cannot have oneself and some other individuals very closely connected to oneself as relata.

(4*) Although *spontaneous* sympathy and benevolence are partial and favour those individuals who are close to oneself in some fashion, this partiality can be corrected. This is because these attitudes are based on empathy which, as an act of imagination, can be voluntarily controlled and governed by reflection. Self-concern stands in need of similar correction, in particular, to prevent it from being temporally too myopic. This is argued in 3.1–3.3 by way of countering the opposing views of Paul Bloom and Jesse Prinz. Schopenhauer also dissents from my view in so far as he asserts that the insight that spatio-temporal individuation is illusory 'is not to be forcibly arrived at by intention or design' (1966: I, 404). But his view will not be examined in detail since, as indicated in 3.4, it is hard to make sense of because of its reference to the influence of the will-in-itself behind the spatio-temporal veil.

(5*) Contrary to what Schopenhauer thinks, positive feelings—of pleasure, joy, etc.—exist in their own right. Therefore, we can experience sympathetic joy along with compassion, and benevolence can be a desire to improve the lot of others not just by removing their negative feelings, but by producing positive feelings in them. But compassion is spontaneously stronger than sympathetic joy, and the spontaneous desire to remove suffering is stronger than the desire to benefit others positively. This psychological asymmetry could lead us to think that morality is also asymmetrical in favour of the negative, but this is a temptation that should be resisted. Chapter 4 is devoted to these topics.

It may be asked: why this interest in examining Schopenhauer's doctrine that compassion is the basis of morality when the manifest claims that constitute it are in need of replacement or extensive revision? The reason is that it is plausible to take an empathy-based attitude, like compassion, to be the centrepiece of morality, and that many moral theories do so. Utilitarianism is the best known example: it takes something like benevolence to play this role. Benevolence raises the same issues of how it relates to the distinction between oneself and others, and to justice; of the extent to which it is possible to overcome the partiality by which it is spontaneously hampered; and of whether removing badness has a special moral weight, as negative utilitarianism regards it as having. Therefore, even if Schopenhauer's nomination of compassion as the core moral attitude is not optimal, the conclusions which you could reach by investigating how it plays this role could be of interest outside the context of the Schopenhauerian morality.

However, there is also a more particular reason for interest in Schopenhauer's ethical theory. This reason is that it construes its core moral attitude of compassion as a means to ascetic self-renunciation: 'moral virtues are a means of advancing self-renunciation, and accordingly of denying the will-to-live' (1966: II, 606). Being unambiguously expressed by him, this claim, examined in 3.4, is part of his manifest moral position. (Shapshay characterizes this as a 'canonical' (2019: 23) or 'traditional' (2019: 25) view among Schopenhauer scholars.) All the same, I am reluctant to place this claim alongside the claims (1)–(5), since it is far from clear how a denial of the will could be an aim of a morality based on compassion. If universal compassion is effective as a means of denying the will, it seems that moral motivation will extinguish itself, since if we cease to will, we cannot will that things go well for others. Consequently, it is not felt to be a lacuna that this thesis does not figure in *The Basis of Morality*.

Yet Schopenhauer does not seem to recognize any problematic tension between moral motivation and the denial of the will. In this respect his teaching appears to be in harmony with Buddhism and perhaps religious ethics in general: they often honour ascetic saints as moral ideals. It will be explored in 3.4 whether the solution to this conundrum in Schopenhauer's case could lie in the fact that the will denied is not just one's individual will but the will that is objectified in as others as well. The breaking of such a will would mean the end of suffering for others, too, and this is a plausible moral goal. However, as will be shown, the denial of such will is a highly problematic phenomenon in terms of Schopenhauer's metaphysics. Thus, the quest for a reasonable interpretation of the thesis that compassion is a means to a higher moral goal of asceticism ends in failure.

Since both the ideals of universal compassion and self-renunciation are exceedingly demanding ideals, the book ends with arguing in Chapter 5 that such demandingness is not an objection that undermines the validity of ideals.

2
Morality and the Distinction between Oneself and Others

2.1 An Ambiguity in Parfit's View

I have suggested that while sympathy or, strictly speaking, benevolence, is a central motive for moral action, it cannot be the only motive, since a sense of justice motivates moral action as well, and it is not derived from benevolence. But it is also the case that benevolence stretches beyond the bounds of morality because we are benevolent towards ourselves, i.e. concerned about our own well-being for its own sake, though how we handle our own well-being is beyond the province of morality, as it is conceived by common sense. Granted, we would not ordinarily say that we are 'benevolent' towards ourselves or, for that matter, that we 'sympathize' or 'empathize' with ourselves, but our anticipation of, for example, the pain and suffering that the near future might have in store for us often enough involves imagining them, and this is likely to make us sad or apprehensive, and to activate our self-concern. Also, as already mentioned, we speak of self-pity. To treat yourself badly can be irrational or stupid, but not immoral as long as the effects on others are bracketed. If not taking good care of yourself had been immoral, taking good care of yourself would have been moral. But this is what an egoist is motivated to do, and Schopenhauer is surely right that such motivation is '*without moral worth*'. Moral concern is concern about the welfare of others for whom things can be good or bad; self-concern is outside the bounds of morality.

However, I shall now argue that things are not as clear-cut as they seem at first sight: there is benevolent concern for individuals who are not identical to ourselves which resembles self-concern so much that it does not qualify as moral concern. The present chapter is dedicated to elucidating both the resemblance between this concern and self-concern and the difference between them and ordinary concern for others which qualifies as moral.

In *On What Matters* (2011: vol. 1) Derek Parfit develops a version of Henry Sidgwick's 'dualism of practical reason' which consists in there being two kinds of reasons to care about the well-being of individuals: *self-interested* or *personal* reasons to care about our own well-being, and *impartial* reasons to care about everyone (else's) well-being.[1] He concedes to Sidgwick that he 'rightly claims that we have reasons to be specially concerned about our own future well-being', but, he goes on, 'many' of these reasons 'are provided, not by the fact that this future will be *ours*, but by various psychological relations between ourselves as we are now and our future selves' (2011: 1, 136). Notice that this suggests that *some* of our reasons to care about our future are provided by the fact that it is *ours*. Similarly, he writes that Sidgwick 'overstates' the rational importance of personal identity (2011: 1, 136), which again suggests that it has some rational importance. This seems to contradict his famous claim in *Reasons and Persons*, pt. III, that 'personal identity is not what matters'.

Apparently, it is not that he has *abandoned* this claim about personal identity, for in a paper published the year after the first two volumes of *On What Matters*, he re-affirms his allegiance to it (2012). After having argued that the animalist or biological view of our identity—according to which are identical to our human organisms—is not true, he confesses that he has 'a reason to *wish* that Animalism were true' (2012: 27), since this would make it easier for him to vindicate his claim that our identity does not matter. Contradicting what is suggested in *On What Matters*, he writes that 'though we have reasons for special concern about our future, these reasons are not given ... by the fact that this will be *our* future' (2012: 27). So, some sort of double-thinking or ambivalence about the importance of personal identity is going on. To resolve this ambivalence, I suggest that we better give up

---

[1] (2011: 1, sect. 19). Parfit writes 'everyone's well-being' (2011: 1, 136)—which includes our own well-being—but it is doubtful whether this is consistent with his claim that we are morally permitted to give 'even greater weight to some stranger's well-being' (2011: 1, 139) than our own.

the view that self-interested reasons are based, even partly, on beliefs about our identity.

As regards the psychological relations that provide us with reasons to care about ourselves, Parfit claims that we have 'partly similar relations to some other people, such as our close relatives, and those we love' (2011: 1, 136). Thus, these relations provide us with '*personal* and *partial* reasons to care about the well-being of ourselves and those to whom we have close ties' (2011: 1, 136). These reasons are 'only *very imprecisely* comparable' (2011: 1, 137) to impartial reasons, reasons to care about *anyone's* well-being. They are only very imprecisely comparable in the sense that, though we can tell, for instance, that we are permitted to save our own lives rather than the lives of at least two strangers, we cannot give anything like a precise answer to how many strangers we are allowed to sacrifice to save ourselves. According to Parfit, this imprecision is due to the fact that, whereas impartial reasons are *person-neutral*, self-interested and partial reasons are *person-relative* in the sense that they 'are provided by facts whose description must refer to us' (2011: 1, 138), either because these facts concern *our own* well-being, or the well-being of people to whom *we* have close ties.

There is, however, an important difference between self-interested and partial reasons as well. Self-interested reasons *permit* us to give somewhat greater weight to our own well-being in comparison to the well-being of strangers but, as Parfit points out, it would be 'too egoistic' (2011: 1, 139) to maintain that they *require* us to give greater weight to our own well-being: we are permitted to 'give equal or even greater weight to some stranger's well-being' (2011: 1, 139) than to our own. However, as he notes, there is in this respect a difference between reasons to care about our own well-being and the well-being of others to whom we have close ties. For in a case in which I could save either my own child or the child of some stranger 'I ought morally to give priority to my child' (2011: 1, 141).[2]

---

[2] But notice that, even though we are not allowed to sacrifice a close friend to save a stranger, we are apparently allowed to sacrifice the friend to save ourselves and to sacrifice ourselves to save a stranger, which would yield the same outcome. For instance, when chased by a hungry lion, we are allowed to outrun a friend, foreseeing that this will mean that the friend is killed by the lion, even though we

This difference seems sufficient for holding our self-interested reasons to be a different kind of reason than the partial reasons that we have as regards others to whom we have close ties. The latter seem to be especially strong *moral* reasons—reasons that are stronger than impartial reasons—with respect to the well-being of others to whom we have close ties, but our reasons to care about our own well-being cannot likewise be especially strong *moral* reasons. If they were, it seems that we could not be *morally* permitted to sacrifice our own greater well-being for the sake of a smaller benefit to a stranger. Consequently, keeping apart self-interested and partial reasons is advisable.

Thus, whereas Parfit lumps together self-interested and partial reasons as person-relative reasons and talks about *two* kinds of reasons (e.g. 2011: 1, 138), we better separate these and talk about *three* different categories of reasons of beneficence: *self-interested, partial, and impartial reasons*. In making his claim about the imprecise comparability between person-relative and person-neutral reasons, he stresses the divide between self-interested and partial reasons, on the one hand, and impartial reasons, on the other hand. I have elsewhere (Persson, 2021) argued that this claim sits ill with his reductionism about personal identity in *Reasons and Persons*, but shall not rehash this argument here. Instead I shall focus on a divide between self-interested reasons, on the one hand, and partial and impartial reasons, on the other hand, which seems to imply that the latter differ by being moral reasons. In other words, it is seemingly implied that the distinction between what concern for well-being falls within or outside the province of morality runs along the distinction between oneself and others. This is apparently in tension with Parfit's reductionism about personal identity in the third part of *Reasons and Persons*.

There he contends that his reductionism can pave the road for an extension of morality into the intra-personal sphere of prudence. He considers 'a boy who starts to smoke, knowing and hardly caring that this may cause him to suffer greatly fifty years later' (1987: 319–20). In such cases in which an individual undergoes considerable psychological change, but there are nevertheless enough of the

---

follow this up by choosing not to outrun a stranger who is chased by another hungry lion. However, we are hardly allowed by common-sense morality to save ourselves, e.g. by pushing our friend (or even a stranger) into the paws of a hungry lion.

psychological relations requisite for identity, he proposes that we may outlaw such great imprudence by importing moral reasons into the intra-personal sphere, with the result that 'we ought not to do to our future selves what it would be wrong to do to others' (1987: 320). But this is incompatible with the quoted claim in *On What Matters* that we are morally permitted to give 'even greater weight to some stranger's well-being' than our own. This permits us, for instance, to commit ourselves to a more painful death to save some stranger from a less painful death, even though we predict that our future self will resist this treatment, while we are hardly permitted to save one stranger from a less painful death at the expense of committing another non-consenting stranger to a more painful death, other things being equal.

I shall suggest a different ground for the distinction between prudential and moral reasons of beneficence than the distinction between ourselves and others, a ground that is consistent with reductionism about personal identity. This ground implies that our reasons to care about the well-being of some people to whom we are not identical, but to whom we have close psychological ties, are similar to reasons to care about our own well-being in a way that rules out that they are moral reasons, whereas our partial reasons to care about the well-being of some other people to whom we also have close psychological ties are like our impartial reasons to care about anyone else's well-being in a way that makes both of them moral reasons.

But this ground also functions as a ground for another type of reasons than these *reasons of beneficence*, namely, what can be called *reasons of justice*. The latter are clearly moral reasons. Irrespective of whether partial reasons are reasons of beneficence or of justice, they can be stronger than impartial reasons of the same kinds. The fact that morality includes reasons of justice explains why morality cannot be imported into the intra-personal domain even if reductionism is true, since we do not have such reasons with respect to ourselves, as will emerge in 2.3.

2.2 Well-Being Accessed from the Inside and the Outside

In order to see that we can have the same sort of reasons of beneficence towards some other people as towards ourselves if Parfit's reductionism is true, we need to take a quick look at the purport of his reductionism. It maintains that our identity consists in the holding of psychological and/or physical relations that can hold to a greater or lesser degree, and there are cases in which it is *indeterminate* whether or not they hold to such a degree that it can truly and definitely be said that we persist. This is a claim about the *analysis* of our identity. But his reductionism also features a claim about its *importance*, expressed by the slogan that 'personal identity is not what matters'. What matters in identity is rather 'psychological connectedness and/or psychological continuity, with the right kind of cause' (1987: 214). The right kind of cause is normally the persistence of one and the same brain.[3]

Psychological *connectedness* is constituted by the presence of psychological connections like persisting memories and desires, while psychological *continuity* consists in *chains* with links consisting of a sufficient number of such psychological connections. This means that psychological continuity could stretch over periods of a person's life between which there is no psychological connectedness. But a substantial reduction of psychological connectedness that is abrupt could make it either indeterminate whether or not the same person persists, or definitely false. To illustrate such changes, we might need to have recourse to science-fiction examples, like those in which a nefarious neurosurgeon manipulates somebody's brain by replacing a major portion of their memories with different memories, and similarly with their desires and other psychological features.

Now even if there are chains of strong enough psychological connectedness for psychological continuity to obtain, there might not be identity. Parfit maintains that this could in principle happen if we imagine that the two hemispheres of a brain each is capable of sustaining the psychology of a person, and they are separated and successfully transplanted into two different bodies (1987: ch. 12). In such cases of *branching* psychological continuity, personal identity is annihilated, he argues, since the original person cannot be identical to both of the resulting persons, who are clearly distinct from each other, and it would be arbitrary to identify the original person with any one of them. Accordingly, personal identity consists in *non-branching* psychological continuity, with the right kind of cause.

---

[3] For my own view of what our identity consists in and whether it matters, see e.g. (2005: pt. IV), (2016), and (2017: 3.1).

But Parfit claims that the occurrence of such a division would not necessarily be *worse for us* than survival as the same person with the same degree of psychological connectedness sufficient for psychological continuity. So, it is the latter relations that matter for us rather than personal identity.

If this is correct, it raises the question how we could be morally permitted to sacrifice ourselves for a smaller benefit to some stranger but never to sacrifice someone else who is closely related to us. For surely we must be morally permitted to sacrifice people who come into being when our psychological continuity branches no less than ourselves. The relations that matter are in both instances the same, according to Parfit. Thus, we find that our reasons to care about some people to whom we are not identical are of the same kind as our reasons to care about ourselves. It follows that these reasons cannot be based on our identity.

On the other hand, although the two post-transplant persons who come into existence when our psychological continuity branches are close to us, our relations to them must be relevantly different from our relations to other people who in our daily lives are close to us, like family and friends. For we can be morally permitted to sacrifice the post-transplant persons to benefit strangers in circumstances in which, according to common sense, we are not morally permitted to sacrifice friends or family members. Therefore, the relations that ground our reasons for concern for the branch-persons must be significantly like our relations to ourselves in the future and unlike the relations that ground our reasons for concern about people who are close to us in everyday circumstances. What are these different relations?

The bases of our reasons for concern about ourselves and branches of ourselves are similar in that, I hypothesize, we are likely to *anticipate*—and, as a result sympathize with—experiences like the pain that any of the branches will feel in the near future in the same way as we anticipate the pain that we ourselves shall feel in the near future. My hypothesis is that such anticipation involves projecting into the future the continuity of consciousness that we experience while we are awake without interruption. On the basis of remembering the continuous flow of our consciousness in the past up to the present, we imagine it running on until it contains the future pain. Thus, our imagination approaches this future pain 'from the inside', by having our consciousness so to speak furrowing a tunnel into the future through which it can flow. This *approach from the inside* is thus an imaginative extension of our introspective access to our current experiences, and it evokes our sympathy with the individual imagined to suffer the pain. By contrast, when we imagine feeling the pain that we believe e.g. someone before our eyes to feel—even if it be somebody close to us—our act of imagination is usually elicited by our observing *outward signs* of pain, such as writhing, grimacing, and screaming.

The non-identical people whose well-being we access from the inside, as in the case of the branch-people, I shall call our *successors*. They are people who spring from us in ways that make them resemble us closely psychologically and frequently physically as well. For the most part these people *replace* us, like the branch-persons described: we cease to exist when they begin to exist. But as we shall soon see, replacement does not necessarily occur, and I count as our successors all those who spring from us in the fashion indicated, regardless of whether we cease to exist when they begin to exist. Our imagination reaches out to the well-being of our successors from the inside, and for that reason they are within the domain of identification and prudence like ourselves. A pair of branch-people will, however, have to access the mental life of each other from the outside.

Other individuals with whom we are familiar in everyday life may also spring from us—like our children—or they may closely resemble us, like our monozygotic twins, but then they do not spring from us in ways that produce the close psychological continuity of our successors. Since we do not generally cease to exist when these others spring from us, they more often *coexist* with us, exist alongside us. These coexisting individuals include ones who are emotionally close to us, as well as strangers. In fact, they include all sentient beings other than ourselves who actually exist. I shall call them our *coexisters*, though they include not only people who are our contemporaries, whose existence at least partly overlaps with ours in time, but also those who exist entirely after we have existed, without being our successors, and who would have been our coexisters had we continued to exist.[4] As will show up, one

---

[4] They could also include our 'predecessors', those whose existence predates our existence, but we can leave these aside since, with the possible example of people who have left things behind with respect to which they have expressed a will, we cannot affect them for better or worse.

and the same individual can be our successor at one time and our coexister at another.

So, we imaginatively approach the experiences of our successors from the inside. These acts of imagination occur spontaneously and are more vivid if the experiences are expected to happen in the nearer future, while they take more of a voluntary effort to be vivid if they are thought to happen after longer intervals. This is due to our *bias towards the near* (future), to which we shall have occasion to return later in this section.[5] By contrast, in general we imaginatively approach the experiences of coexisters from the outside, though there are conceivable qualifications. For suppose that one of your functioning hemispheres is successfully transplanted to a body that is a replica of your body, save that it has no hemispheres (or only one hemisphere which is not the seat of any psychology). If your body and the remaining hemisphere go on existing and constitute a psycho-physical person, that person is arguably you (as I suggest, e.g. in 2017: 86). When you look ahead to the transplant of one of your hemispheres, the person who will receive it will be a successor of you, but later, when the transplant has occurred, this person will be one of your coexisters. Consequently, one and the same person may first be a successor of yours, then a coexister, but the person is not a coexister of you at the time when imagination from the inside can occur.

However, in exceptional circumstances you could imaginatively approach the experiences of someone from the inside at a time when that person coexists with you. Suppose that you have for a period of time been hooked up to the nervous system of another individual in such a way that you will share all the bodily feelings of this individual—feel the pains, itches, the hunger, thirst, and so on, located in this individual's body—whereas this individual will not share your feelings. Then, if you were to hear that this individual will soon experience pain, you would be likely to imagine from the inside what this will be like, just as you would if you were to hear that you yourself will feel pain soon. This is because you will feel this pain occurring in another body just like you feel the pain that occurs in your body. But there is still a reason for saying that the pain is only this individual's,

---

[5] Parfit discusses this bias in (1987: pt. II), and I do so in (2005: ch. 15).

not yours as well, because it is located in this individual's body. If there are no efferent links connecting you to this body, so that you cannot move it at will as you can move your own body, and if you do not see with the eyes or hear with the ears of this body, it could reasonably be denied that it is your body, though you feel bodily sensations in it. It would then be true that you feel someone else's pain because you feel the pain in their body.[6]

Such fantastic cases aside, we can imaginatively approach from the inside the experiences of other people only if they succeed us, just as we imaginatively approach our own future experiences, while the experiences of those who coexist with us or exist in the future without succeeding us are approached from the outside. The approach from the inside is conducive to identification with the target, as it is the approach we customarily adopt to ourselves in the future. Plausibly, this is something that could place our successors within the realm of prudence along with ourselves.

The outside approach faces more hurdles than the inside approach. Others often have overt properties that hinder imagining what they feel and sympathizing with it. These factors can broadly be divided into two categories. First, there are those factors that prevent our imagination receiving enough concrete material to start up. Examples are if other beings are known to us merely by sketchy descriptions rather than by being present to our senses in good observational conditions, or if they are members of a large crowd rather than being present to our senses individually. A counterpart to this sort of obstruction in the case of the inside approach is anticipation of what we might feel in the distant future rather than in the more imminent future.

Other hurdles in the path of the outside approach are of a more 'tangible' sort. They are features that we dislike and that make us dislike those who exhibit them. Examples are properties that strike us repulsive, such being ugly, noisy, smelly, and exhibiting harmful behaviour towards us. These tend to make us turn away from bearers of them before our empathy has time to get going. They contrast with

---

[6] I discuss this case in (2005: 314–20). This thought-experiment shows that Schopenhauer's idea mentioned in 1.3 that we could feel suffering both 'as our own' and yet 'in another person' makes literal sense, though for other reasons than his.

properties that we find attractive, such as being cute or beautiful, and displaying charming or beneficial behaviour.

In the case of some features, it is difficult to tell whether they belong to the first or second category. Consider beings whose looks and behaviour are so dissimilar to ours or unfamiliar to us that there is not anything in them that we recognize as signs of their suffering. It may be that these features merely prevent our empathy from getting a grip, but it is also a fact that what is unfamiliar may make us react negatively, whereas familiarity breeds liking. There is something called *the exposure effect*, a tendency to grow to like what we come across regularly. Also, if we perceive someone as having an attractive appearance, we are prone to attribute other positive features to it, such as having a friendly or congenial character, whilst if we perceive someone as ugly, we are prone to attribute other negative features to it, such as being stupid or insensitive—as though the fact that we do not spontaneously empathize with them were due to there not being much to empathize with.

Features that we dislike are features that we are averse to being exposed to. Whether this aversion spreads from a feature to the subject possessing it seems to depend on whether we see the feature as belonging temporarily and accidentally or more permanently and essentially to the subject. Thus, suppose we countenance somebody who is dirty and bad-smelling because they have just been pulled out of a marsh. Then, although we dislike these novel features of them, we do not immediately start disliking them and maliciously want them to suffer because of their obnoxious stench. Their stench and bad hygiene must be a more permanent feature of them for this to be likely to happen.

It might be suggested that if these features are more permanent, it is more probable that their subjects are *responsible* for having them. It may be that we tend to hold subjects responsible for their features under these circumstances, but I do not think that attribution of responsibility is necessary for the spread of disliking. For example, I believe that people's dislike of the sliminess of slugs could make them dislike slugs so that they maliciously want to hurt them, though they would hardly regard the slugs as responsible for their sliminess. It is probably true that if people make it perfectly clear to themselves that slugs are not responsible for their sliminess and, so, that they do not deserve ill treatment because of it, their malevolence would subside, or not arise in the first place. But as long as they do not consider the issue of the slugs' responsibility for their sliminess and what they might deserve in virtue of it, their dislike of sliminess could be freely transferred from the property to its bearers.

I believe that we have here come across a ground for the attitude of malice or malevolence and the attendant emotion of *schadenfreude*. As adumbrated in 1.3, we are not malicious or malevolent when we want to harm individuals to the extent that we think that they deserve to be harmed, and it is not *schadenfreude* we feel when we feel pleased or satisfied for the reason that they are harmed to this extent. Nor is malice to be equated with desiring to harm individuals to an extent that we regard as undeserved. Malice is desiring to harm beings independently of considering whether this is just or justifiable.

To understand why we start desiring to harm individuals without considering whether this is just or justifiable, attention should be called to the fact that we are malevolent towards individuals who we take to have harmed or negatively affected ourselves or someone with whom we identify. In such situations, as mentioned in 1.3, we are liable to acquire immediately a desire to harm excessively these individuals in return because our spontaneous empathy with ourselves and those who are close to us is usually disproportionally strong. If we then learn that the perpetrators of the harm have suffered a harm whose absolute magnitude satisfies our exaggerated desire that they be harmed, we are immediately pleased, without pausing to consider whether this magnitude matches what they deserve, or is justifiable for some other reason.

We may believe, reasonably or not, that we or those who are close to us have been unjustifiably harmed, though we do not believe that there is any agent of this instance of unjustifiable harming. For example, we may believe that we are unjustifiably worse off than people who are congenitally more good-looking, though we do not believe that we have thereby been treated unjustifiably by anyone. Nevertheless, we may envy the others their good looks and maliciously wish that they become disfigured and feel *schadenfreude* if we learn that this has happened.

As regards our approach from the inside to our own future experiences or the experiences of successors like the branch-persons, the obstacle is rarely the acquisition of disliked properties which make us dislike our future selves or successors, since normally no changes dramatic enough for this reaction will occur in the foreseeable future. Due to the exposure effect, we are disposed to like ourselves as we currently are because we have normally been roughly the same for some time. The most frequent obstacle here is instead our bias towards the near future. This bias makes us discount our more remote future, so that, for instance, we are relieved when future suffering is postponed, and disappointed when future enjoyment is postponed, even though we do not consider this to make them more improbable. It usually takes considerable voluntary efforts to imagine our own experiences in the more remote future anything as lively as we spontaneously imagine our own experiences in the immediate future.

So, I conjecture that, some science-fiction cases aside, our relationship to someone is moral just in case our imagination reaches out to their well-being from the outside, and prudential just in case it reaches out to it from the inside. This is a distinction between two methods of imagining what goes on in the mind of someone other than ourselves at present and, thus, two means of representing to ourselves reasons for caring for and promoting their well-being, reasons of beneficence with respect to them. One method is naturally applicable to our coexisters whom we perceive from the outside, as their existence is parallel with ours, the other method to our future selves and successors who continue our conscious existence at the present time, often after the interruption of a period of unconsciousness, like sleep. We have noted, however, the theoretical possibility of accessing from the inside the well-being of coexisters, for example, those with whom we have been hooked up. For reasons that will emerge in 2.3, our concern for these individuals qualifies as moral (these reasons have to do with the fact that their will is independent of our will). It would seem misleading to describe the output of these two procedures as a dualism of kinds of reasons, as Parfit does following Sidgwick, since we are dealing with only one kind of reason—reasons of beneficence, reasons to be concerned about someone's well-being for its own sake—which we access by two routes.

As indicated, the approach to someone's well-being from the inside can be defective not only by the bias towards the near coming into operation. Especially if we consider ourselves in the more distant future, we may have undergone such drastic changes, physically or psychologically, that we dislike ourselves as we have become. But since we do not *perceive* these disagreeable features, as we frequently do with respect to coexisters, our dislike of our future selves or successors on the basis of these features would likely be less strong. It may also be softened by the fact that we empathize with the latter from the inside.

We can of course also be misinformed about the experiences of our future selves or successors. If this happens, it could make our attitudes to them irrational or badly informed, but not immoral. It could, however, be morally wrong *of others* to let us act on the basis of such attitudes; it might be that we morally ought to be paternalistically restrained if our behaviour is significantly harmful to ourselves or our successors. It is morally permissible for others to allow such harmful treatment of our future selves or successors to take place only if we satisfy the conditions of autonomy, conditions such as being free, well-informed, and rational.

Consequently, the wider intra-personal domain of prudence—which includes our successors as well as ourselves—is not entirely sealed off from moral intrusion. Morality can be invoked when people are thought to be less fit to look after their own interests, or the interests of their successors, than some of their fellow-beings are. Moral protectionism or paternalism justifiably kicks in when somebody's well-being is not clear-headedly accessed from the inside. But it is hard for others to be sure that they know better and are more concerned about what is good for people than the people themselves, unless these people go to the extreme of exhibiting 'great imprudence' (to quote Parfit). Notice, however, that since my account does not imply that our concern for our future selves is based on personal identity, the adoption of reductionism about it could not reduce self-concern and increase the risk of imprudence. There is, then, no need for extending morality into the realm of prudence and, as will transpire in 2.3, there is another kind of reasons than reasons of beneficence—namely reasons of justice—that prevents such an extension.

It is often held that a principle of autonomy to the effect, roughly, that we are morally permitted to act as we please in so far as nobody but ourselves is concerned as long as we meet the conditions of autonomy, of being well-informed, rational, and free, is a moral principle. Such a principle, however, differs from the principles of beneficence and justice in that the motivation to act in accordance with the principle of autonomy is not *moral* motivation, and there is no moral motive for interfering with those who are in the process of implementing autonomous decisions because they cannot contravene morality.

It may be asked: is it a necessary condition that psychological continuity connects us to a future individual in order for our imagination to be able to reach this individual's well-being from the inside? There is psychological continuity in the discussed cases of division because the hemispheres underpinning the psychological connectedness between the original person and the branch-person(s) are the hemispheres of the original person. But, as I have argued in earlier work (for instance in 2017: 83–4), identity of the brain-parts underlying psychological states is not necessary for there to be continuity between them, or their being elements of the same consciousness. However, there is no need to argue this point now, since a case can be made for thinking that psychological continuity is not necessary for us to have imaginative access from the inside to the experiences of some future individual.[7]

Suppose that you are told by someone trustworthy that sometime after you have gone to sleep tonight, the elementary particles composing your body will fly apart, but that a fraction of a second later other particles will come together to compose a body similar in every macroscopic respect to your body as it was when it dissolved. Owing to this perfect physical similarity, the mind of the person popping into existence in your bed almost straightaway will be indistinguishable from your mind as it was at the time when your body was dissolved. The gap during which there will not be anything like you in your bed might be so short that our senses could not register it, but even such a minuscule gap of non-existence is enough to rule out that the person popping into existence will be numerically the same person as you. For there is nothing to guarantee that you are identical to this person rather than any other indistinguishable person that may pop us elsewhere in the universe at the same time, no traceable link that could not obtain in

---

[7] Again, I have presented the following sort of case a number of times before, most recently in (2017: 85–6).

relation to any other of these possible persons. Nor will this person be psychological continuous with you, since this presupposes some kind of continuity in respect of the physical basis of consciousness, although this may not amount to any identity of brain-parts. In addition, we might stipulate that you are informed that this has happened on a number of occasions in what you have hitherto regarded as *your* past, the past of one and the same person, but which you must now realize is a series of numerically distinct, qualitatively identical persons popping into existence.

Will you then be able to access your successor's experiences from the inside? This kind of act has clearly been possible on a number of occasions in the past while people laboured under the illusion that the person waking up tomorrow was identical to them, but will they be able to do so when this illusion has been dispelled? I think so if (1) they are convinced that it is as certain that their replacements will be in the same condition as they currently are when they will be replaced as they are about the condition of their future selves when they survive in the ordinary fashion, and (2) they keep in mind how quickly the replacements will occur. The chief psychological function of some continuity of the physical basis of the mind is to ensure us that there will in the future be a mind more or less exactly like ours at present. The information that the replacement has occurred successfully a number of times in the past should be able to perform the same function. If the coming replacement also goes well, this should further strengthen the belief in the person popping up that the replacements will go well in the future, too.

(2) rules out that the bias towards the near gets a chance to kick in. In circumstances in which it does kick in, we need to reflect that, despite being further in the future, the experiences of the replacements are nonetheless no less real, and on the basis of this insight make voluntary efforts to imagine them in order to raise them to a higher degree of vividness and stability, as will be discussed in 3.2.

I have suggested that when we imagine having experiences from the inside, we use the memory of our stream of consciousness flowing from the past to the present that we experience whenever our consciousness is uninterrupted. The experiential nature of this source does not stop us from using this procedure when we imagine experiences from which we are separated by a period of unconsciousness, such as the experiences we shall have when we wake up tomorrow. If so, the fact that during the considered period of unconsciousness there will be a gap of non-existence so brief that it cannot be registered by our senses should not be sufficient to stop our imagining the future experiences from the inside, given that we are as certain that they will occur as we would be if this gap had not occurred. Thus, I shall include our replacements under the circumstances considered among our successors and count them as 'springing' from us, since it is true that they would not have existed had we not ceased to exist. Psychological similarity with individuals who are related to us in this loose sense is enough to enable us to imagine their experiences from the inside.

2.3 Reasons of Justice, and Coexisters

A general difference between our successors and coexisters is that the latter typically have wills, or capacities for having desires, that are *largely independent of ours*, and frequently literally oppose ours when they are our contemporaries. By contrast, our successors have wills that are largely dependent on our present wills because of the manner in which they spring from us: they will will the same as we now will, or what we now want them to will. This dependence, which they share with our future selves, is especially extensive when our successors are close to us in time, while it usually decreases in the course of time. But a salient difference is still that in the case of our coexisters, the individuals with the independent wills are individuals *with clear (bodily) boundaries which separate them from us*, whereas a later stage of a successor with a will comparatively independent of ours will not be clearly distinct from earlier stages whose wills are more dependent on ours because these stages share the same body. Thus, our coexisters are subjects with wills independent of ours, and with definite boundaries that separate them from us. It has in 2.2 been established in addition that, some fantastic cases apart, their well-being is approached from the outside, whereas the well-being of ourselves and our successors is approached from the inside.

The independence of the wills of our coexisters means that as a rule our harmful treatment of them will be morally permissible only if we get their *autonomous consent*. With the sanction of such consent, it is morally permissible to do to them what it is morally permissible to do to ourselves and our successors, e.g. to sacrifice them to save others. In the absence of such consent to our treatment, it will be harder morally to justify this; for example, it will take greater gains in terms of benefits.

The existence of coexisters actualizes problems of *just (or fair) distributions* of benefits and burdens between them and us. These problems arise as the result of the independence of the wills of our coexisters and their (bodily) separateness, but they are aggravated when these wills are implemented in actions that create conflicts over useful resources. For instance, our coexisters may treat us badly, and thereby provide us with reason to regard them as *deserving* to be harmed in return. Or they may acquire unowned natural resources, and thereby acquire *rights* to an exclusive use of them, which correspond to *obligations or duties* on our part to leave their property alone. Or we might shoulder obligations and duties to them by making promises to them, or accepting favours from them. There are many different accounts of what constitutes justice, some of them denying the existence of deserts and rights in favour of a more egalitarian conception of justice, but this is a matter that cannot be pursued now.[8]

In contrast to the factors obstructing moral concern already considered, factors like deserts and rights are designed to be morally relevant. If somebody really deserves to be treated badly, or has a right to less, this necessarily supplies a moral reason to treat them accordingly. It might be, and has been, disputed whether deserts and rights exist, but if they do exist, they are necessarily morally relevant. In opposition to this, the problem with the distinction between beneficiaries who are present to our senses and those who are known merely by vague descriptions is of course not whether this distinction can really be drawn; it is that it appears obviously morally irrelevant. Likewise, it seems obvious that the fact some beneficiaries are members of a large crowd whereas others present themselves to us as single individuals cannot morally justify greater concern for the well-being of

---

[8] Also, reasons of justice frequently assume a deontological rather than a consequentialist form to the effect, e.g. of taking our reasons not to violate rights as being more stringent than our reasons not to let them be violated, whereas reasons of beneficence are more often construed as consequentialist.

the latter. As soon as we become aware that our differential concern or discrimination depends on these grounds, we tend to recognize it as indefensible.

I have referred to the exposure effect, that we grow to like and be concerned about that to which we are accustomed from experience and which has served us well. This liking and concern can be transferred to similar items and, thus, engender more liking and concern for them than for items whose appearance is markedly different. If we are brought to realize that we might have grown to like the dissimilar things as much had we been as much exposed to them, and that, in any case, being accustomed to the appearance of something is no reasonable ground for liking it, we are in a position to see that this attitudinal mechanism is unfounded.

Contrariwise, we are disgusted by beings who are disfigured or bad-smelling. As was suggested in the preceding section, it is not necessary that individuals are held responsible for having these features in order for the disgust to spread from the features and infect the individuals themselves, and generate a malicious desire that they be harmed. But the thought that they are not responsible for the properties and, therefore, do not deserve ill treatment on the basis of them creates a rift between the property and the subject that is liable to prevent the infection. In the absence of more palpable grounds, the disliking of individuals who are, e.g. disfigured might be justified by fanciful measures such as the doctrine of *kharma*, according to which ugliness is the outcome of responsible wrong-doing in an earlier existence.

Turning to grounds for dislike for which ascription of responsibility is more plausible, individuals are often responsible for their hostility towards us, and then they may be thought to deserve our hostility in return. If people are responsible for being richer than us, they may also be responsible for miserly hanging on to their wealth without sharing it with others. In our eyes, this may make them deserving of ill treatment in return. On the other hand, when it is obvious that people have acquired their wealth through a stroke of good luck—e.g. by luckily having found gold or oil—their wealth is readily perceived as undeserved and unjust.

There are, then, a number of factors that obstruct our empathy and sympathy with coexisters from the outside, some of them resulting not simply in callousness, but in our desiring to harm them, either because we see this as deserved or justified, or because the conditions of malice or malevolence are fulfilled. On the other hand, there are also a number of factors that facilitate our empathy and sympathy with coexisters: we have grown to like them because we have had a lot of positive exposure to them, or their appearance strikes us as attractive or similar to ours. It is not hard to see that some of these factors are apt to make our empathy and sympathy with coexisters unjustifiably biased or partial.

Some have taken this to show that these attitudes are not fit to play a central moral role but, as will be argued in Chapter 3, this is a partiality that can be rectified by rational reflection. On the basis of such reflection, we can be motivated to make a voluntary effort to imagine more lively the feelings of those whose feelings we are not spontaneously inclined to imagine—ideally as lively as we spontaneously imagine our own feelings in the immediate future—and discard as morally irrelevant features for which individuals are not responsible, or which have nothing to do with their level of well-being.

An appeal to justice can then figure in our reflections on our (lack of) empathy and sympathy with our coexisters. By contrast, reasons of justice are inapplicable if we are dealing only with ourselves and our successors. Whilst reasons of beneficence necessarily support our taking up an attitude of sympathy and benevolence towards individuals and benefiting them for their own sake, considerations of justice could tell us to make them worse off. They could tell us that we have been too generous to those to whom we are close at the expense of other coexisters, and that we should rein in our benevolence towards them. Contrariwise, they could tell us that we have been too hard on those towards whom we spontaneously feel antipathy and should rather benefit them. But then we would benefit them *because this is just*, not simply for the reason that it is good for them. This is why reasons of justice can act as checks on our reasons of beneficence, and reasons of justice can be reasons to adopt negative attitudes of anger and indignation just as well as positive attitudes of gratitude.

Reasons of justice can be either partial or impartial. We have an impartial reason of justice to respect everyone's property, but partial reasons to those to whom we have special relations, for instance, to those to whom we have made promises, or to children that we have brought into existence, or to people whose lives we have endangered, or to people who have done us favours. Such partial reasons justify our giving special attention to particular individuals.

Apart from such partial reasons, we are spontaneously bent to be especially concerned about the well-being of some of these people who are close to us, and to hold our reasons of beneficence with respect to them to be especially strong. This is often unjustified, and due to our having imagined how they feel more vividly than how strangers feel, but it may also be justified by adding impetus to our partial reasons of justice. That sympathy with the individuals involved motivates us to act in accordance with reasons of justice is indicated by the fact that we are much more inclined to act on such reasons when we ourselves are at the receiving end of injustice (witness, e.g. the reaction of children when they themselves get the smaller piece of chocolate rather than someone else getting it, even if it be a sibling). When we care little about the well-being of those at the receiving end, reasons of justice will often not suffice to move us to action. If we concretely imagine how they will feel, reasons of beneficence could offer supplementary motivation. Additionally, as remarked in 1.2, if we imagine *ourselves* through bad luck ending up in a position similar to that of the victims of injustice, this is likely to strengthen the motivational power of reasons of justice. But this is not an exercise of empathy and sympathy.

It should, however, be noted that there are two reasons why we may be more upset by an inequality of well-being when we ourselves are the worse off party than when other individuals, especially strangers, are this party. It may indeed be that we represent our own well-being more vividly than the well-being of others. But it may also have to do with our being more inclined to see such inequalities as more unjust because we exaggerate our own deserts or rights. This could be a manifestation of the so-called *overconfidence bias*, the tendency to think that we are better than we actually are in various favourable respects, better in our profession, as parents, lovers, drivers, and so on.

As a rule, we cannot have reasons of justice as regards our successors or future selves—to the effect that our treatment of them is just or unjust—because their wills are not sufficiently independent of our wills, and there are no definite boundaries between them and us to guide distributions of benefits and burdens. It is true that the relation we have to our successors is analogous to the relation we have to our children in that we bring these individuals into existence, and it is this which provides children with a right against us to be given special care. But by definition, our successors resemble us so much more than our children that it makes no sense to shoulder the role of care-givers of our successors. Besides, we cannot shoulder this role because our successors as a rule replace us, whereas our children's existence usually overlaps with our own. In special circumstances, we could, however, develop relations to our successors that will give them rights against us, or us rights against them, as will now be seen.

Consider again the thought-experiment in 2.2 in which, after the separation of my hemispheres, only one of them is taken out and transplanted into another duplicate body, whilst the other hemisphere remains connected to my body. If it is right to hold that I am identical to the person with my original body, minus one hemisphere, the person with the other hemisphere in a duplicate body will after the transplant be a coexister of me, though he will be a successor of me as long as I now look ahead to the separation of one of my hemispheres and the transplantation of it.

Let us call the post-transplant person with both my body and one of my hemispheres 'Newme', and the person with the transplanted hemisphere 'Exme'. It would be implausible to claim that the difference between these persons, which makes one of them identical to me, could make it morally permissible for me to sacrifice Newme to save you, but not to sacrifice Exme. More plausibly, I would be permitted to sacrifice Exme no less than Newme, though Exme is a distinct person from me, but quite close to me. This is in line with the claim that in the original division case it would be morally permissible for me to sacrifice either of the post-transplant persons, neither of which is identical to me, just like it would be to sacrifice myself. But whereas these persons would just be successors of me at present, Exme will be a close coexister of me later when I have become Newme, even though I earlier had access from the inside to Exme's experiences no less than to Newme's experiences. Thus, I could be morally permitted to sacrifice a future close coexister of me for a stranger, just as I could be permitted to sacrifice myself or a successor of myself.

Newme could develop relations to Exme that would impose on him special obligations towards Exme. For instance, Exme could do Newme a favour, which would give Newme reason to regard Exme as deserving favours in return. Or Newme could promise to treat Exme in some manner. Immediately after the transplant, Newme's and Exme's wills will be exactly alike, but in the course of time they are likely to become more and more dissimilar. When they start existing, however, Newme would be permitted to treat Exme like I would now be permitted to treat him, or Newme who is my future self. But since Exme is a coexister of Newme, Newme's treatment of Exme is a *moral* matter, to which reasons of justice apply. Newme's treatment of Exme could be morally wrong, whereas my present treatment, or planned treatment, could not.

Therefore, at least in some special circumstances, it appears to make no difference whether the treatment of someone is a moral or prudential matter. It does not follow that we are morally permitted to treat near and dear people who surround us in everyday life as Newme would be morally permitted to treat Exme in these circumstances. For these people have wills that are much more independent of and unlike our wills, and we are likely to have developed relations to them that provide us with partial reasons of justice with respect to them. This makes it indispensable to ask for their autonomous consent to proposed treatments.

I could then have moral relations and reasons with respect to Exme in the future, albeit he is a successor of me now. At present I could also imaginatively approach his well-being from the inside. Therefore, this sort of approach to someone's well-being does not rule out that their well-being could matter morally to us, even though in all but science-fictional cases the approach to well-being that morally matters is solely from the outside. Another exception to this rule is presented by the thought-experiment in 2.2 with another individual to whom you are attached by afferent links. Here, too, there is an inside approach to the well-being of somebody who matters morally. But generally when our approach to someone's well-being is from the inside, their will is dependent on our will, or on the dependent will of some successor(s) of ours, from which they are not separated by definite (bodily) boundaries, though they may be so separated from us.

To sum up, prima facie it appears that morality regulates our concern for the well-being of others, whilst our concern for our own well-being falls outside its scope. By arguing that the persistence of branches of us, who are not identical to us, can be as good for us as our own survival, Parfit in effect undermines the idea that the boundary between what is within morality and what is not follows the boundary between ourselves and others. For concern for the well-being of our successors like the branch-people falls outside morality, just like concern for the well-being of ourselves. The concern that morality regulates must rather be concern for others who coexist with us, or exist in the future without being our successors. These are the sorts of numerically distinct individuals that we come across in everyday life. Since we do not come across any successors, it is not strange that we commonly believe that *all* others fall within the realm of morality, and that it is only the self that is outside of it.

I have suggested that our relations to our coexisters and our successors typically differ in two significant ways. First, we typically, but not necessarily, access the well-being of our coexisters from the outside, whereas we access the well-being of our successors from the inside, like the well-being of our future selves. Generally speaking, concern generated from the outside is weaker, though our concern for our selves in the distant future may be quite weak. Secondly, the wills of our coexisters are more independent of our wills, so they are more likely to disagree with us about distributions of benefits and burdens; and when our coexisters exist simultaneously with us, they can oppose us in action, as they are bodily distinct. These circumstances raise issues about what a just distribution of benefits and burdens consists in. The reasons of justice generated can be either partial or impartial, and they belong to morality, as opposed to prudence. When our successors have wills that are more independent of ours, they usually exist in the more remote future, and their wills will then be dependent on closer successors of ours, from whom they are not clearly distinct. This means that it would be difficult for our reasons of justice to get a firm grip on them.

In 1.1 I claimed, in opposition to Schopenhauer, that the sense of justice is independent of compassion and other empathy-based attitudes and that it does not consist simply in an aversion to harming. It can now be seen that nonetheless the application of reasons of justice is in practice coextensive with the application of reasons of beneficence when they are supplied by access to well-being from the outside.

We get the fullest imaginative representation of someone's well-being when we can approach it from the inside, and it is the well-being of an individual in the near future. (The representation of our own *present* well-being is not based on imagination, but on actually experiencing it and, as a consequence, it is the most vivid.) This is how we represent the well-being of ourselves and our successors in the near future. It should function as a yardstick when we assess the adequacy of the outside approach to the well-being of close and alien coexisters. The assessment that this process yields could be impartial reasons of beneficence as strong as self-interested and partial reasons of beneficence rather than the latter being much stronger, as commonsense morality apparently allows.

It is, however, not part of the objective of this book to investigate whether there are any grounds other than those of justice that could morally justify more concern for the well-being of some beings than others. I have insinuated that a number of grounds employed to justify more concern for the well-being of some cannot reasonably be held to be valid. Similarly, I have argued that the fact that somebody's well-being is one's own is not anything that in our eyes could justify special concern about it, since we cannot reasonably be less concerned about the well-being of our branches than our own. But this leaves open the possibility that some other properties in our possession could justify special self-concern, which will not be pursued here.

2.4 Schopenhauer on the Metaphysics of Compassion

The fact that I have disposed of our identity as a justificatory ground enables me to escape a predicament in which Schopenhauer finds himself when he tries to explain how compassion with the suffering of another is possible. Due to the fact that he apparently believes that 'another's suffering can directly become my motive' (1995: 148) only if I somehow represent it as *my own*, he is led to the problematic view that in order for compassion with another's suffering to be possible, I must '*feel it as my own*, and yet not *within me*, but *in another person*' (1995: 165). He might understand this double-sidedness to mean that, although a higher degree of compassion necessitates realizing that spatio-temporal individuation is an illusion that hides the real identity and oneness of everything, it does not make compassionate people entirely oblivious to this individuation. A rough analogy might be a perceptual illusion, like seeing a stick half-immersed in water. It looks bent to us, and this might make us feel some inclination to believe that it is bent, but this inclination is held in check by our knowledge that it is not bent. Similarly, compassionate people could represent the suffering that is the object of their compassion as the suffering of another in the spatio-temporal world, though they realize that in reality this individual is not distinct from themselves.[9]

As was seen, e.g. in 1.3, Schopenhauer's account implies, first, the Kantian view that space-time is something that our cognitive faculty imposes on reality and, secondly, that the undivided reality beneath this imposition is something that could evoke our compassion, namely a 'will', though it does not necessarily go with consciousness as does willing in the ordinary sense. The first claim is at least quite contentious, but the second is downright incomprehensible, as will now be argued.

Schopenhauer takes even inanimate nature to be an objectification of the will, but this cannot imply that inanimate nature is a possible object of compassion, for this object must be something that is conscious of such things as suffering. Sometimes he hints enigmatically at the possibility of a consciousness which is not consciousness *of* anything, though he admits that we cannot picture 'a *not unconscious* state except as one of *knowing* which... carries within itself... the

---

[9] Colin Marshall (2020: 1.3) points out that Schopenhauer held there to be multiple Platonic ideas corresponding not just to species of things, but to individual beings; hence, to this extent there could be diversity that is independent of space and time. He quotes Schopenhauer thus: 'it follows from this that *individuality* does not rest solely on the *principium individuationis* and so is not through and through mere *phenomenon*, but that it is rooted in the thing-in-itself, the will of the individual' (1974: II, 227). However, these ideas are '[n]ot themselves entering into time and space' (1966: I, 129), so they cannot enable us to perceive others 'to be distinct *spatiotemporal individuals*' (Marshall, 2020: 7) and, consequently, cannot help accounting for our compassion for *particular* individuals distinct from ourselves. On Schopenhauer's conception, an idea 'stands in between' particular things and the will as thing-in-itself because it 'has not assumed any other form peculiar to knowledge as such, except that of representation in general, i.e. that of being an object for a subject'; therefore, it is 'the most *adequate objectivity* possible of the will' (1966: I, 175). There are indefinitely many 'grades' of this sort of objectification of the will corresponding to the grades of development of kinds of things in the world. They 'form a pyramid, the highest point of which is man' that contains all lower kinds (1966: I, 153). Only the highest kinds have ideas corresponding to their individuality but, he adds, how far down the roots of this individuality go 'is one of those questions I do not undertake to answer' (1974: II, 227; cf. 1966: I, 131–3).

separation into subject and object, into a knower and a known' (1974: II, 274). Still, he thinks it possible that 'through death...we are...shifted only into the original state which is *without knowledge*, but is not for that reason absolutely *without consciousness*' (1974: II, 274). But even if there were such states of consciousness—contrary to what he maintains elsewhere: '*consciousness* consists in knowing, but knowledge requires a knower and a known' (1966: II, 202)— they could not arouse compassion, for they could not consist in a subject being conscious of an object like suffering, since it is consciousness for which 'the contrast between subject and object vanishes' (1974: II, 274).

Consciousness with a subject-object structure is '*individual consciousness*' which 'is not conceivable in an *immaterial or incorporeal* being, since...consciousness, knowledge, is necessarily a brain-function really because the intellect manifests itself objectively as brain' (1974: II, 273). Consciousness, thus conceived, 'is extinguished by death' (1974: II, 273). An episode of such consciousness could consist in a subject being conscious of suffering, so to this extent it is suited to be an object of compassion, but it will be the consciousness of one individual among others; therefore, Schopenhauer's problem how this suffering could motivate anyone but the subject feeling the suffering remains. Compassion is necessarily directed at subjects who are conscious of objects—suffering, etc.—but such subjects can be found only in the spatio-temporal world of distinct individuals. According to him, awareness of the fact that these subjects are all objectifications of the same will could enable one subject to feel compassion for another subject, but this fact of will-identity does not imply that their *consciousnesses* are united, and it is consciousnesses with subject-object structure at which compassion must be oriented.

So, the crucial question is: how could the consideration that other conscious subjects suffering are objectifications of the same will-to-life as I am boost my motivation to relieve their suffering to something like the level of my own suffering? Alongside identity and the relationship to successors, the fact that I am linked to somebody else by the afferent pathways envisaged in 2.2 could make me feel their present suffering and, thereby, enable me to imagine from the inside their imminent suffering. But the connection of being objectifications of the same will could hardly conduct feelings from one consciousness to another.

What is requisite is, then, some sort of unity or sharing of consciousness, not (just) unity or sharing of will. We might be misled by the ordinary meaning of 'will' to think that the will as conceived by Schopenhauer is also accompanied by consciousness and knowledge, but this is not so. He says of 'knowledge, and the determination by motives which is conditioned by this knowledge' that 'this belongs not to the inner nature of the will, but merely to its most distinct phenomenon as animal and human being' (1966: I, 105), thus, subjects of consciousness and knowledge necessarily have the diversity and multiplicity of inhabitants of the spatio-temporal world of phenomena. They remain diverse and multiple as such subjects even if they happen to be objectifications of one and the same will, and the object of compassion is the suffering of such subjects.[10]

Schopenhauer maintains that 'we know and understand what will is better than anything else' (1966: I, 111; II, 318). This is because will is what we allegedly *are*, so the knowledge of it is *immediate*, 'without any form, even the form of subject and object, for here knower and known coincide' (1966: I, 112). There are several problems with this assertion. To begin with, the fact that subjects of knowledge, like

---

[10] Schopenhauer is ambiguous on the relation between consciousness and will. When he affirms that consciousness 'manifests itself objectively as brain', he appears to place it on a par with the will because it, too, manifests itself in our bodies. But he hastens to add that consciousness is 'psychologically' 'secondary' relative to 'the will that is alone the primary and everywhere the original thing', just as consciousness is 'physiologically' 'something secondary, as a result of the life-process', in particular the life-process of brain-function (1974: II, 273). Now this expresses a different hypothesis of the ground of consciousness: not that consciousness *manifests* itself in brain-function, but that it is the *result* of such a function which is a manifestation of the *will*, 'that it is at bottom tertiary' (1966: II, 278). This is a hypothesis that sits ill with his (transcendental) idealism, according to which a brain is something represented and, thus, dependent on consciousness. Thinking that consciousness in turn is dependent on the brain causes him to make paradoxical claims like 'the body exists only...in the brain' (1966: II, 259, 271). What Schopenhauer should have said is rather that the will somehow produces consciousness for which the will then appears as various objects, spatio-temporally and causally ordered, i.e. the will is thus objectified. It is not the brain that produces consciousness, though it may be that of the will which is objectified as brain that does this. Our will is objectified in our whole organism, and he claims, surprisingly, that brain-damage is not enough to change our character (1966: II, 246), though it obviously affects our consciousness.

ourselves, are identical to something does not imply that they have any knowledge of what it is to which they are identical—let alone knowledge that is immediate in the sense of lacking subject-object structure, a structure that we have just seen that Schopenhauer elsewhere affirms to be inescapable. Suppose that we grant him that 'the subject of knowing... appears as an individual only through his identity with the body' (1966: I, 100). Our identity with our body still gives him no warrant for claiming that we have 'double knowledge of our own body', not just 'as representation, but as something over and above this, and hence what it is *in itself*' (1966: I, 103).

Further, he holds that 'the body is the condition of knowledge of my will... I cannot really imagine this will without my body' (1966: I, 102). Consequently, since my knowledge of my body has not been shown to extend beyond representations, the same goes for my knowledge of my will. A confinement to representations of knowledge of the will is confirmed by other remarks of his. He accepts that we are aware of our will in the form of time: 'I know my will not as a whole... but only in its individual acts, and hence in time' (1966: I, 101; cf. II, 198). But this knowledge must be spatial, too, as 'the act of will and the action of the body... are directly *identical*' (1966: II, 248), and the body 'exhibits the... will spatially' (1966: I, 334). Therefore, it has not been shown that we have any knowledge of either our body or will that transcends representations and grasps anything as it is in itself.

In fact, we are aware of our willing, wanting, desiring, striving, etc. only as something that involves feelings, thoughts, etc. motivating us—all elements of consciousness that he writes off as not belonging to 'the inner nature of the will'. Consider pain, an impression that is 'contrary to the will' (1966: I, 101). Remove from the experience of pain the impression itself, which is felt as located somewhere in the body, and the fact that it motivates an avoidance reaction. Nothing seems left that could plausibly be characterized as knowledge of 'the inner nature of the will'. What about 'mere resolves of the will'? No, they are 'a matter of the intellect alone', 'until they are carried out' and become 'inseparable from doing' (1966: II, 248). The claim that self-consciousness provides knowledge of the will is then fraught with troubles.

It has been suggested by Bryan Magee (1983: 144) that we should understand the will as the thing-in-itself as an unspecific 'force' or 'energy'. But Schopenhauer rejects this to be tantamount to that 'we have in fact referred something more unknown to something infinitely better known' (1966: I, 112). Besides, 'force' and 'energy' are concepts that are 'abstracted from the phenomenon' (1966: I, 112) and, thereby, unfit to characterize the thing-in-itself.

By insisting that the thing-in-itself can be conceptualized as will, he stresses that 'the inability to know the thing-in-itself is modified to the extent that the thing-in-itself is merely not absolutely and completely knowable' (1996: II, 197), but may have aspects 'which for us are absolutely unknowable and incomprehensible' (1996: II, 198). Okay, but the problem is to understand what information is supposed to be imparted by conceptualizing the thing-in-itself as will, i.e. what is supposedly knowable about it. It is *entirely* obscure to me what the will as thing-in-itself is thought to be and, thus, how the insight that the will is what everything that exists is an objectification of could buttress compassion with other sentient beings.

There is something of a dilemma here: if the will as thing-in-itself is conceived as something that makes it more plausible to say that everything that exists—including inorganic things—is an objectification of it, the harder it appears to be to understand how it could buttress compassion, whereas this *may* be more comprehensible if only sentient beings are assumed to be objectifications of the will. For it might be suggested that if, say, we think of the will as something running through all sentient life-forms in virtue of the fact that they all share the same evolutionary origin, making this idea lively to ourselves could serve to bridge the palpable differences between sentient beings and facilitate imagining their feelings. Granted, but this will be imagination from the outside, and for Schopenhauer compassion with the suffering of another takes to '*feel it as my own*' (1995: 165), that is, to imagine the suffering from the inside, if not actually feeling it.

In any case, it is preposterous to maintain that the everyday emotion of compassion commits us to something as abstruse as it does on Schopenhauer's analysis. Moreover, by construing compassion as an extended egoism to the effect that 'the non-ego has to a certain extent become the ego' (1995: 144), the status of compassion as a moral motive is jeopardized since, by his own admission, when a motive is egoistic, it is 'consequently *without moral worth*' (1995: 143). But it would be too strong to object that this construal *undermines* the moral status of compassion because extended egoism is after all different from ordinary egoism by not excluding others. On the other hand, this difference must not preclude that the extended ego's well-being could possess something like the motivational power of the ordinary ego's well-being. In any case, better to deny the rational and moral importance of identity than its existence, as I have argued.[11]

Other attempts than my Parfit-inspired proposal have been made to drop the metaphysical cargo of Schopenhauer's account. As an alternative to the standard metaphysical interpretation, Shapshay advances an 'axiological interpretation' of his account of compassion: 'I (the compassionate person) recognize intuitively that the suffering other and I matter (morally speaking) in a similar way' (2019: 179). But it is hard to see how this could plausibly be an alternative *interpretation* of what Schopenhauer actually says about how compassion is possible. For his explanation contains undeniable reference to the Kantian view that space and time are forms of our cognitive faculty, so that the plurality and diversity of individuals exist only in our representations and not in reality itself. In reality, there is instead an identity to the effect that 'My true inner being exists in every living thing' (1995: 210) because we are all objectifications of the same will. On this account, compassion is 'certainly astonishing, indeed, mysterious. In fact it is the greatest mystery of ethics' (1995: 144). His explanation of this mystery is relegated to a 'supplement' of his essay on the basis of morality, which is avowedly devoted to expounding a 'metaphysical explanation' of this basis. None of this makes any sense if

---

[11] There is a further complication on which I shall not dwell: Schopenhauer's idea of *eternal justice*, according to which 'in all that happens or indeed can happen to the individual, justice is always done to it. For the will belongs to it' (1966: I, 351). This idea, if correct, would complicate his account of all-encompassing compassion, since the fact that it is just that someone suffers counteracts feeling compassion for them. The idea of eternal justice is, however, quite implausible. If the individual who intentionally causes harm and the individual who suffers it had really been identical—in so far as they are both objectifications of the same will-to-life—considerations of justice would not be applicable, as I have argued in this chapter. But if the consciousness of the former is distinct from the consciousness of the latter—which is compatible with them being objectifications of the same will— such considerations may be applicable, but then the idea that the infliction of harm is just rather than unjust is undercut.

Schopenhauer had had in mind the making of a moral claim such as Shapshay's.

There is, however, another way of understanding her, not as putting forward an interpretation of what he foremost had in mind as much as a proposal about what he *should* have had in mind, a *replacement* for his metaphysical account which has the virtue of scrapping its metaphysical load. This is as how I view my own account. However, in contrast to my account Shapshay's axiological account does not solve the problem that Schopenhauer rightly assumes that an account of compassion must solve, namely to explain how the suffering of another could motivate us more or less as much as our own suffering. My account accomplishes this, not by denying the distinctness between us and the other, but by denying that it matters and, thus, needs to figure in the content of the empathy which undergirds compassion. But, so far as I can see, Shapshay does not offer any explanation of why a recognition that the value of another is similar to our own value should make it motivate us to a similar degree. It does nothing to meet the objection 'Yes, but it is still the value of *another*', i.e. the objection that there is a cleft between oneself and another to be motivationally bridged. Without such an explanation, it has not been ruled out that recognition of a similarity in respect of value is a purely cognitive attitude which is completely emotionless and motivationally idle. Then it would not be a moral attitude according to Schopenhauer's empirical method on which the moral must be motivational. Consequently, Shapshay's axiological interpretation would drop compassion as a basis of morality along with the metaphysical cargo.

Moreover, although the moral claim that is embedded in Shapshay's axiological interpretation, 'The suffering other and I morally matter in a similar way', is a claim that appeals to many, Schopenhauer would hardly be among them. This claim to the effect that *beings* morally matter similarly should be distinguished from 'The *suffering* of another and my *suffering* morally matter in a similar way'. If the latter is shorthand for 'The suffering of another that is as bad for this individual as my suffering is for me morally matter in a similar way', it fits in well with Schopenhauer's express view that goodness and badness are 'essentially relative' (1966: I, 360). The latter judgement does not imply that the other and I morally matter in a similar way because *we* have the same value in ourselves; it is compatible with both of us having *no* value. It is possible that the fact that something satisfies or frustrates the will of some being creates something of positive or negative value for this being, though this being has no value in itself, that what has positive or negative value is simply the satisfaction or frustration of a will. However, on this construal of the axiological claim, too, there is the problem about how the fact that something is as bad for another as it is for me could be morally equally important in a sense implying that I am motivated to the same extent—the problem that his metaphysical explanation is designed to solve.

Shapshay's axiological interpretation is however wedded to the view that 'all sentient beings... have positive, inherent value' (2019: 176); it involves a recognition that 'the other has positive inherent value, at bottom, just in the way that I have inherent value' (2019: 180). But I can find nothing that documents that Schopenhauer would accept this view; on the contrary, his rejection of the idea that anything could have 'absolute worth' seems clearly to commit him to a repudiation of it. Shapshay maintains that by this rejection he asserts only that '"worth" is a comparative term' (2019: 177), but in fact he asserts in the same breath that worth 'is *relative*, in that it exists *for* someone' (1995: 95) because it involves a 'relation to a desiring will' (1966: I, 362). If this is right then, by her own admission, her axiological interpretation is a 'non-starter' (2019: 178).

Let me, however, try to clarify why Schopenhauer thought that compassion with the suffering of another requires extended egoism to the extent that we feel the suffering of the other as our own. I believe that we find a clue in the following passage in which he explains egoism: it 'is due ultimately to the fact that everyone is given to himself *directly*, but the rest are given to him only *indirectly* through their representation in his head; and the directness asserts its right' (1995: 132). I interpret this as affirming that our own suffering is something that we *actually feel*, whereas the suffering that we think others might have is suffering that we have to *imagine* feeling. The remark that 'the directness asserts its right' could then mean that only actual feelings could motivate us, or could motivate us to a significant degree. But that it is actually felt by us is true only of our suffering *at present*; the suffering that *we* might feel in the future is also suffering that we have to imagine. Consequently, if his diagnosis of egoism was on the right track, it would be limited to the present, but this is evidently untenable.

It is, however, true that the suffering that we actually feel is as a rule more vivid than the suffering that we imagine feeling, and that its motivational power is therefore greater. I have called this tendency our *bias towards the perceived* (2005: 183). In so far as this is what Schopenhauer means by 'the directness asserts its right', he has a point. But although our spontaneously imagined feelings are generally less vivid and, thus, exercise less motivational influence on us than actual feelings, we can by voluntary effort make our imagined feelings more vivid and, thus, boost their motivational power, as I shall argue in 3.2. If this is so and if, as I have argued in 2.2, the fact that these feelings are had by ourselves does not figure essentially in what is imagined, it is not necessary that it is we ourselves that are believed to be the subjects of the imagined feelings that could motivate us significantly. To fight our egoism it could therefore suffice if we imagine having the suffering that we believe others to have and by voluntary effort make this imagining livelier. It is not necessary—what a thought-experiment in 2.2 showed to be in principle possible—that we actually have the feelings of somebody else in order for them to be motivationally effective for us, just as we do not have to have in the present the feelings that we believe we might get in the future—which is not possible even in principle—in order for them to be motivationally effective.

Simple creatures are capable of desiring that their present sensations of pain stop. These creatures do not have any conception of themselves as subjects of experience, so it must be the character of the sensations in themselves rather than the fact that they are owned by subjects with certain features that motivates them. Imagining feeling pain (or pleasure for that matter) is using material derived from such sensory experiences. When evolution equipped creatures with a capacity to imagine pains in advance of having them, it is most likely because such imagining could motivate them just like actually having the sensations themselves, even if it does not motivate to the same degree because imaginative representations are less forceful. But sensations motivate without involving any conception of their subject.[12]

---

[12] As Thomas Nagel writes: 'The desire to be rid of pain has only the pain as its object' (1986: 162).

Therefore, Schopenhauer goes wrong in thinking that the pain and suffering of another can evoke compassion and a benevolent desire to alleviate them only in subjects who enter a state in which the pain and suffering turn out to belong to themselves. Imagining a 'bare' subject, without any specific properties conducive to elicit empathy and compassion, being in pain and suffering could call forth these reactions. But then it is doubtful that he could be right in thinking that malice 'makes its ultimate aim the *pain* of another' (1995: 145, his emphasis). If imagining a bare subject having the feeling of pain gives rise to an intrinsic desire to eliminate the pain imagined—just like the sensation of pain gives rise to an intrinsic desire to end the sensation—it cannot also give rise to an intrinsic desire to prolong it. Such prolonging is the job of sensations of pleasure and imaginary representations of them. It is true that when we are malicious or malevolent, we want someone else to suffer, but we want it for the reason that we think, however confusedly, that this individual possesses some disliked property that makes us dislike him or her. By contrast, when we are benevolent towards somebody, there might not be any property for which we like them in particular. Should there be such properties, they will rather give our benevolence a boost.

In this connection it is important not to let Schopenhauer's conception of positive feelings as consisting in the disappearance or absence of negative feelings confuse matters. He writes:

> Our immediate sympathy is not stirred by the good fortune or pleasure of another *purely as such*, as it is by the suffering... and misfortune of another *purely as such*. If, even *for ourselves*, our activity is stirred only by our sufferings... whereas a state of contentedness and prosperity leaves us inactive and in idle unconcern, how could it not be just the same in regard to others? (1995: 146–7)

Certainly, if he were right about the non-existence of positive experiences, we would have to be stirred by negative experiences only, regardless of whether we imagine their subjects to be ourselves or others. But, as will be emphasized in Chapter 4, positive experiences of pleasure and joy exist just as negative experiences of pain and suffering, and we are stirred to promote our own good fortune and pleasure purely as such, just as we are stirred to prevent our own misfortune and suffering purely as such. I would echo Schopenhauer's question: how could it not be just the same in regard to others? When we are stirred to promote the misfortune of others and prevent their good fortune, this is because we attribute to them properties that make us dislike them, which is just what we do in our own case, though here such attributions are more uncommon. Just as the imagined pain and suffering of ourselves as such never stir us to prolong them, so the imagined pain and suffering of others do not do so, as allegedly happens according to his construal of malice.

It is beyond the scope of this book to examine any closer than has already been done what are the properties that are disliked and liked. Some of these properties may be more or less tenuously associated with reasons of justice. Human beings are also easily convinced that those to whom they ascribe positive properties have other positive properties and that those to whom they ascribe negative properties have other negative properties. For example, they may slip into assuming that there is not much to empathize with in case of those who are ugly because they are stupid or insensitive as well. Such associations may be pervasive in the societies in which we grow up and may be so firmly inculcated on our minds that it is difficult for us to liberate us from them later in life, though their intrinsic plausibility is scant. As a rule, we start believing in such associations not because of their plausibility, but to be accepted by groups to which we are eager to belong, and often continue to believe in them for the same reason.

As remarked earlier, I shall not systematically scrutinize the tenability of any putative reasons of justice, either. Common-sense morality recognizes reasons of justice that are fit to single out particular individuals as being specially deserving or having special rights. The question whether such a morality can be upheld or has to give way to a more impartial and egalitarian morality is beyond this book's scope.

3
The Partiality and Moral Importance of Empathy

3.1 Bloom and Prinz' Attack on the Moral Importance of Empathy

Paul Bloom has argued at length that empathy is essentially and inescapably partial or biased. It

> is a spotlight focusing on certain people in the here and now. This makes us care more about them, but it leaves us insensitive to the long-term consequences of our acts and blind as well to the suffering of those we do not or cannot empathize with. Empathy is biased, pushing us in the direction of parochialism and racism. It is shortsighted, motivating actions that might make things better in the short term but lead to tragic results in the future. It is innumerate, favoring the one over the many. It can spark violence; our empathy for those close to us is a powerful force for war and atrocity toward others. (2016: 9)

In other words, empathy is not a reliable guide to or ground for moral actions and reactions because it is directed first and foremost at individuals who we know well or who are present before our eyes at the expense of those who are strangers to us, or beyond the reach of our senses and known only through vague descriptions. With respect to individuals at its focus—including ourselves—it is especially focused on how they will fare in the more immediate future. Its focus is on what is temporally close as well as spatially close. Furthermore, even among those who are present to our senses, some may not easily be the target of our empathy because they are different from us in some conspicuous ways: their skin colour is different, they are disfigured, smelly, etc. Finally, empathy is 'innumerate': we cannot empathize with groups of people in proportion to their number. The larger the group, the more of a drawback this limitation is. These limitations—familiar by now—may lead to empathy contributing to aggression and violence towards those outside its reach.

Jesse Prinz voices similar objections to empathy as a moral tool: it 'may lead to preferential treatment', 'may be subject to unfortunate biases, including the cuteness effects', 'is prone to in-group biases', 'is subject to proximity effects', and so on (2011a: 226; cf. 2011b: 227–30).

Bloom understands empathy to be 'the act of feeling what you believe other people feel – experiencing what they experience' (2016: 3). Prinz' conception is similar: 'it's feeling what one takes another person to be feeling' (2011a: 212). As should be clear by now, this is not how I construe empathy, which is as *imagining* (what it is like) feeling what you believe another is feeling. Empathizing with another is surely not *feeling* what you believe others to be feeling. For instance, when you empathize with somebody who you believe to be feeling physical pain, e.g. because they have hit their thumb with a hammer, you do not actually feel physical pain. With a greater or lesser degree of liveliness, you imagine feeling a pain like the one you believe they are feeling, a feeling that you probably take to resemble what you yourself have experienced in the past in similar circumstances.

This raises the well-known problem of knowledge of other minds: how you know what other beings experience or, indeed, whether they have any experiences at all. For what enables you to imagine adequately certain feelings is that you remember or have learnt from experience what it is like to feel them, or something resembling them. But how do you know that what you name, e.g. 'burning pain' is anything like what somebody else names the same? If it is significantly different, it is questionable whether you can be described as empathizing with them when they feel their so-called burning pain.

Granted, it would be too strict to demand that empathizing with someone requires succeeding in imagining feeling something which is *exactly* similar to what this individual is in fact feeling. You may be said to empathize with someone when you imagine feeling as you believe they do, though your belief is only roughly right, say, their suffering is somewhat more intense than what you imagine. As mentioned in 1.2, Adam Smith requires only that what you imagine feeling must not be 'altogether unlike' what they feel, and it would probably be unwise to try to be much more precise. But empathizing surely requires at least imagining having the right *kind* of feeling: for instance, you cannot be said to be empathizing with somebody if you imagine them being glad when they are in fact sad, or being proud when they are in fact ashamed. You cannot even be said to be empathizing with somebody should you be right in imagining them being proud, but you are completely mistaken about the object of their pride: say, if the object of their pride is having finished a novel, and you think that it is having lost weight, though you need not know what more precisely it is about having finished the novel that makes them proud (cf. Smith, 1790: I.i.1).

The best way to deal with the problem of how close the match between what we imagine feeling and what someone is actually feeling for us to count as having empathized with this individual's feeling might be by distinguishing between higher and lower grades of empathy, and leaving it open what the bottom level is. But this is only one of two seemingly intractable problems: the other is determining how close a match we have accomplished in particular cases of putative empathy. We probably have to do this by checking how satisfied the target individual appears to be with the sympathetic or benevolent response elicited by our putative empathy. But it goes without saying that these are issues with respect to which we are out of our depth.

Empathy with somebody implies that the feeling this individual is imagined having is *good or bad* for him or her. For instance, it is odd to talk about empathizing with somebody who is feeling surprised or their mouth to be open if these feelings are neither positive nor negative. It is also odd to say that you empathize if what you imagine is not a feeling but another sort of experience, such as seeing what you believe others are seeing from their points of view, or hearing what you believe them to be hearing. However, if you imagine them seeing or hearing something beautiful or ugly, or seeing dazzling light or hearing deafening sounds, in short if what they are imagined seeing or hearing gives them pleasure or displeasure, there is material for empathy, but this is in virtue of its inclusion of something felt in the shape of pleasure and displeasure. This is anyway a constraint that I would like to put on my use of the term of the term 'empathy'.

Bloom and Prinz' conception of empathy fails to distinguish it from *emotional contagion*: for example, if you are surrounded by sad people, this is likely to make you sad, while if you are met with smiles, this is liable to put you in a good mood by a mechanism that is not fully understood. It seems that observing smiles tends to make us smile which in turn tends to make us cheerful. In these cases, you are actually feeling the emotions that others are having, not imagining feeling them. Bloom notes that emotional contagion is 'not quite the same as' empathy (2016: 40), but he misses the salient differences. Prinz goes even further than Bloom by claiming that 'empathy in its simplest form is just emotional contagion' (2011a: 212).

Some of Bloom's arguments against empathy trade on the failure to separate it from emotional contagion. He correctly points out that we might find ourselves sad without realizing that this is the result of the sadness of others having infected us. Then we are not likely to be motivated to do anything to relieve their sadness: 'Without an appreciation of the source of one's suffering, the shared feeling is inert' (2016: 173). The sadness or whatever feeling emotional contagion infects us with may not be motivationally inert, but since it is we who feel sad, the behaviour it motivates is likely to be self-directed and not altruistic. By contrast, we cannot empathize with someone's sadness without believing that the sadness we imagine feeling is the sort of sadness that we believe this individual to be feeling because empathizing with someone's sadness consists in imagining feeling a sort of sadness precisely for the reason that it is the sort that we believe this individual to be feeling.

Due to the same conflation of empathy and emotional contagion, Bloom fails to see how empathy could enter into concern for somebody. He writes about a case of empathizing with somebody in anguish: 'you see the victim's face contorted in anguish, but you don't see anguish in the consolers, just concern' (2016: 175). However, if you empathize with the anguish of somebody who is terminally ill, say, you do not feel the same anguish over death; instead, you imagine what it would be to feel the anguish over death that you believe this individual to be feeling. Your dominant reaction to imagining this may well be a benevolent concern or desire to ease the anguish of the patient. You may also feel sorry for the patient, but you are unlikely to feel any anguish over death, as you might were you seized by emotional contagion. Therefore, it should not be expected that your facial expression be that of someone who is feeling anguish when you empathize with somebody who is feeling anguish.

Bloom distinguishes empathy from cognitive empathy (2016: 17): 'if I understand that you are feeling pain without feeling it myself' (2016: 17), this is cognitive empathy. Cognitive empathy is 'morally neutral' (2016: 38): people who are morally good share it with 'successful con men, seducers, and torturers' (2016: 37). So, Bloom seems to think—correctly—that cognitive empathy is not enough to motivate moral behaviour, whereas empathy in the proper sense— 'emotional empathy'—can be. The long quotation from him above clearly implies that he thinks that empathy motivates, for his objection to it is that it often motivates us to act wrongly rather than rightly. But he does not tell us what it is about emotional empathy that makes it a motivator in contradistinction to cognitive empathy.

Prinz, on the other hand, adds to the list of accusations that 'empathy is not very motivating' (2011a: 225). But this is hard to square with what he says in support of other accusations of his. As regards preferential treatment, he reports that when subjects had been presented with a vignette about a woman awaiting medical treatment, 'they overwhelmingly elected to move her up at the expense of those in greater need' (2011a: 226; cf. 2011b: 228) who were anonymous to them. And as regards in-group biases, he refers to some studies that have 'found that empathy leads to helping only when the person in need is a member of the in-group' (2011a: 226). But then empathy can after all motivate us to favour or help the people with whom we empathize. Thus, the more plausible moral objection to empathy is not that it is not motivating, but that it is marred by a partiality that tends to lead us morally astray because it *is* motivating.

Bloom rightly distinguishes empathy from sympathy and pity (2016: 40), and from compassion and concern (2016: 40–1)—to which he is more favourably disposed than empathy—though he does not have much to say about how he would like to distinguish between them. He writes that '*sympathy* and *pity* are about your reaction to the feelings of others, not the mirroring of them ... If you feel bad for someone in pain, that's sympathy, but if you feel their pain, that's empathy' (2016: 40). As remarked, the emotional response to empathy need not be of the same kind as the feeling imagined which must be roughly like the feeling of the individual who is the object of empathy. The characterization 'feel bad for someone in pain' would be at least as apt as a characterization of compassion as of sympathy (and pity).

He insists, however, that compassion does not require empathy (2016: 41). This allegedly makes it 'more diffuse than empathy'; as a result, it is 'weird to talk about having empathy for the millions of victims of malaria, say, but perfectly normal to say that you feel compassion for them' (2016: 40–1). Thus, on his view, compassion is not, as empathy, innumerate, and exposed to criticism on this score. But, although I think you can be *concerned* about a million victims, and want to improve their lot, you cannot feel compassion for them, strictly speaking, since you cannot feel compassion for so many *individually*. It is well known that compassion for a single victim before your eyes can be greater than compassion for an anonymous multitude. To my mind, if compassion (or sympathy) is to be a *bone fide* emotion, it must involve empathy with some individual sufferers, and it will thus inherit the defects of empathy. Hence, it is important for me to argue that these defects are corrigible, as I shall do in 3.2.

By contrast, another psychologist, Daniel Batson, takes empathy to entail emotions like compassion, sympathy, and a 'whole range of other-oriented emotions' (Batson, 2019: 29). These emotions, which he labels empathic emotions or empathic concern, also include 'tenderness, soft-heartedness, sorrow, sadness, upset, distress, grief, and more' (2019: 29). It seems to me that Batson's employment of the term 'compassion' is not in accordance with everyday use when he asserts that there is such a thing as 'feeling compassion for the unconscious victim of a mugging, who's feeling nothing at all' (2019: 29; cf. Smith, 1790: I.i.1). We can certainly feel sad or sorry for such a victim, for instance, because we imagine what it would be to have suffered the damages that the victim has suffered, and maybe to wake up with them. But, even in the wider sense recommended in 1.2, this is not compassion unless it involves imagining another's feelings of a negative kind, and feeling sorry as a result. Analogously, being glad for another's sake, e.g. because they died in their sleep and were spared terrible suffering, is not sympathetic joy if no positive feelings that are believed to be theirs are imagined. Therefore, even when compassion and sympathetic joy, along with empathy are understood in the wider, technical manner proposed, they should not be thought of as inclusive as being sad and being glad for someone's sake.

Although Batson acknowledges the acts of imagination that in my terminology constitutes empathy as something which is 'psychologically distinct' from 'the resulting empathic feelings' (2019: 32), it is the latter that 'empathy' designates in his terminology, i.e. he employs 'the terms *empathic concern* and *empathy* interchangeably' (2019: 30).

Over a period of at least thirty years, Batson has amassed a welter of experimental evidence in favour of what he calls the 'empathy-altruism' hypothesis (see Batson, 2012 and 2019). This hypothesis 'claims that only when there's perception of need will empathic emotion produce altruistic motivation because only then is there reason to increase the other's welfare' (2019: 29). The reader may detect a trace of Schopenhauer's focus on the negative in this formulation (albeit Batson does not refer to him), but Batson grants that when 'the other's state is positive', there is something that 'has been called *empathic joy*' (2019: 29). However, when you imagine another's positive state of feeling pleasure, say, this might not only induce you to feel empathic or sympathetic joy; it might also make you altruistically motivated to prolong the pleasure. This could well be motivation whose ultimate goal is 'to increase the other's welfare' which is Batson's definition of altruism (2019: 22).

According to Batson's hypothesis, 'perception of need' is among the antecedents of altruistic motivation. It involves '*seeing a discrepancy between the other's current state and what you think is good for him or her on one or more dimensions of well-being*' (2019: 189). But, clearly, such a discrepancy is not anything that you can literally *perceive* or *see*. Consider another individual's being hungry which might be said to consist in a discrepancy between the current state and the good state of being well fed. You can certainly perceive various events which constitute *evidence* for someone's being hungry, e.g. their queueing up where food is served. On the basis of such behavioural evidence, you could be justified in believing that another individual is hungry, but you do not perceive the hunger or need for food itself—you *infer* it from what is perceived—except in your own case. And we have seen that a mere belief is not enough to motivate compassion and an altruistic desire to feed somebody.

I have suggested that what is necessary in addition is that you imagine feeling the hunger that you believe the victim to be feeing, but Batson has come to deny that this is necessary. His reasons for this denial do not support it, however. He maintains that 'we can actively imagine how another person feels about his or her need and still feel relatively little empathic concern... if we place either little or negative value on the other's welfare' (2019: 195). Granted, but this shows only that imagining how another feels does not in all circumstances produce stronger empathic concern and that it can be counteracted by a negative evaluation of the other's welfare. This is compatible with such imagining playing the role that Batson reserves for 'perceiving another's need', namely to produce empathic concern in conjunction with positive valuation of another's welfare (2019: 194–8) and even simply in the absence of negative valuation of it. None of his reasons tells against this possibility.

The following claim is true, however: 'We can feel empathic concern for someone in need without being instructed to adopt his or her perspective... For many people, an imagine-other perspective seems to be the default' (2019: 196). That is, we spontaneously adopt such a perspective in many circumstances; therefore, we need not be instructed to do so. Nevertheless, as Batson concedes, and his experiments show, 'when inducing empathic concern in the lab', such 'perspective instructions' are useful (2019: 197).

He is also aware of the fact that '[e]mpathy isn't evoked by the needs of nonpersonalized others', for instance '[t]hose we encounter as one of many with similar needs' (2019: 233). Our belief that each and every one in a large crowd is very hungry may be as firm as our belief that a single individual before our eyes is very hungry, and yet it is easier for us to feel empathic or sympathetic concern for the latter, other things being equal. Why is that? It is not because we perceive the hunger more clearly in this case; as already observed, we never perceive the hunger of another. It is instead because it is easier for us to imagine feeling the hunger of a single individual than the hunger of two, let alone a multitude. I take empathy to be this act of imagination which activates sympathetic concern (in the absence of counteracting factors). Batson's experimental evidence is compatible with this interpretation of the empathy-altruism hypothesis.

As implied, he understands this hypothesis as stating that perception of another's need in conjunction with valuing their welfare produce altruistic motivation *by means of* producing empathic emotion or concern (as illustrated by a figure, 2019: 197). But, as indicated in 1.2, I would rather see empathic emotions, like compassion or sympathetic joy, on the one hand, and altruistic or benevolent desires, on the other hand, as two *side-ordered* effects of empathizing with another or imagining how another is feeling, especially but not only when this individual is liked or valued. If we imagine the subjects feeling sad because they think that something bad is happening, or will happen, to them, or afraid because they think something bad might happen to them, without our being able to do anything about it, we shall feel compassion or sorry for these subjects. Thus, our emotional reaction could be the same, sadness or sorrow, even though the negative feelings imagined—sadness and fear—are different. However, to the extent that we believe that we can do something to remove or prevent the emotion-evoking bad events, we shall have an altruistic or benevolent desire to do so. Since it is not unusual for us to think that we can do something to avert such bad events without being completely successful in this respect, we often experience both empathic emotions and altruistic or benevolent desires.[1]

Nonetheless, it should be emphasized that these attitudes do not necessarily accompany each other. For instance, I have elsewhere (2017: ch. 2) argued that we have moral reason to cause the existence of beings who would lead good lives. This provides us with reason to have altruistic or benevolent desires to bring them into existence. But we cannot feel compassion for those who have not yet begun to exist and risk missing out on having good lives, since this is not a loss that we can imagine what it is like for someone to be subject to: in this situation there is not anyone having feelings that we could imagine what it is like to have. Nor can we feel compassion for those who die in their sleep and are deprived of future good life, but we can feel sorry for them since, if we know the good lives they have been leading, we can imagine a continuation of these lives that is cut short. Naturally, this is not possible as regards beings whose lives have not started, but we can imagine these lives starting, and that is enough to have a benevolent desire that they do start if we believe that we can do something to this effect, and to feel sympathetic joy if we imagine these beings being alive and in a happy state of mind.

Of those who deny my claim that we can have moral reason to cause good lives to begin, many would concur with me that we have moral

---

[1] I discuss the nature of desire and emotion at length in (2005: chs. 4–6).

reason to prevent the commencement of miserable lives. But we cannot feel compassion for the non-existent whose lives would be miserable, though we can predict that we would feel compassion for them once they have started to exist. Thus, we should not regard the possibility of having such an other-directed emotion as a *sine qua non* for the presence of moral reasons to act. What is necessary for such reasons is that we could have a benevolent desire that such lives do not begin, and such a desire could be elicited by imagining what these lives would be like when this is something we can affect.

3.2 Spontaneous Empathy and Voluntary, Reflective Empathy

We have seen that a mere belief that an unknown individual is suffering is unlikely to suffice to make us feel compassion and have benevolent concern to relieve the suffering. On the other hand, empathy with sufferers does motivate us to adopt these attitudes. It has already been observed that if that were not so, Prinz and Bloom's case against empathy to the effect that it is a poor guide to moral actions and reactions, since it is biased and innumerate, would be undercut.

It is true that, as Bloom maintains, we 'cannot empathize with more than one or two people at the same time' (2016: 33; cf. Prinz, 2011a: 229). It also true that we find it harder to empathize with people who are different from us in conspicuous ways, such as having a different skin colour, or who are physically repulsive to us, and that this is likely to lead to discrimination, or exclusion of individuals from benevolent concern on morally unjustifiable grounds. Empathy is also biased towards the near future in the sense that we empathize more readily with the suffering that individuals—ourselves in particular—will feel in the near rather than in the more distant future. De Waal sums it up: 'Empathy builds on proximity, similarity, and familiarity' (2010: 211). This is why Bloom—rightly—thinks that 'empathy is a terrible guide to moral judgment' (2016: 45).

On the other hand, he admits that 'it can be strategically used to motivate people to do good things' (2016: 45). The question then arises whether it is not a better strategy to try to discipline empathy than try to do without it. The latter seems to be what Bloom recommends when he claims that 'on balance, we are better off without it' (2016: 39); similarly, Prinz hopes for 'the extirpation of empathy'

(2011b: 228). In my view, this would be throwing out the baby with the bathwater, for the risk is that without empathy we would not be concerned with anyone's well-being, not even our own beyond the present moment. As we have seen, Bloom believes that such concern does not require empathy, but he concedes that so-called cognitive empathy is not sufficient for concern when he writes that people who lack concern could have such empathy, e.g. con men, torturers, and psychopaths. What, then, could fill the slack left by cognitive empathy? As remarked in 3.1, Bloom does not seem to answer this question.

His appeal to compassion is unhelpful because it is biased and innumerate just like empathy: we feel more compassion for suffering that is close in time, for individuals who we know well, who are attractive, and for single identifiable individuals than for masses of anonymous individuals. A readily available explanation of this fact is that empathy is a motivating source of this attitude.

Empathy with someone is capable of motivating because it is imagining what it is like for this individual to have some positive or negative feeling, and this consists in having an 'image' or, better, a sensuous representation of the feeling which is qualitatively similar or isomorphic to the feeling itself, because it is derived from having this kind of feeling. Thus, as Bloom notes (2016: 147–9), to be able to empathize adequately with somebody who is feeling pain, say, it is necessary to have felt a similar pain; so, for instance, those rare individuals who are congenitally insensitive to pain cannot empathize with those who are exposed to pain. Since having pain motivates you to try to rid yourself of it, it is not surprising, as the following reasoning shows, that imagining somebody having the pain that you believe this individual to have could motivate you to try to rid the individual of it, given that the imagined pain is intrinsically similar to an actually felt pain.

The evolutionary explanation of why we so readily imagine feeling a pain that we think that we shall ourselves suffer if we do not take action is surely that this will motivate us to take action to avoid the pain. Then, provided it could serve our reproductive fitness, we should expect that the same device is put to use with respect to our relations to others, so that imagining someone else having a pain could also motivate action to save them from the pain, as both commonsensical experience and experimental evidence bear out. This is feasible because, as shown in 2.2, imagining that a pain will be our own pain is not a part of what motivates us because we could be as much motivated by the pain that we think that branches of us will feel. However, since the imagined pain is not as vivid or forceful as an actually felt pain—unless it is hallucinatory—it will not motivate to the same degree, for it motivates 'in proportion to the vivacity or dullness of the conception' (Smith, 1790: I.i.1.2). A vivid sensuous representation of pain can be more informative about what a pain is like than a verbal description of it can hope to be, as a picture can give more information about something visual than a verbal description; hence, its greater motivational potential.

At a pre-linguistic stage, the belief that another is in pain will have to be expressed in a medium of sensuous representation; thus, there will then be no distinction between so-called cognitive empathy and empathy in the present terminology. You would then be moved to some extent to relieve the pain that you thought the other to be having.

If, as in a thought-experiment in 2.2, you have been hooked up to someone else's nervous system by something functioning like afferent pathways, so you have actually felt the pain this individual feels in his or her body, you would be more strongly motivated to eliminate it, probably as strongly motivated as this individual. But then you could not *empathize* with the pain that this individual is feeling at the present time for the same reason that you cannot empathize with the pain that you are now feeling in your own body. You could, however, empathize as much with the pain that this individual will be feeling in the immediate future as you would do were this pain to be your own. Again, this brings out that the fact that the pain is thought to be your own is not an ingredient in what motivates you.

The reason that you cannot *imagine* feeling a pain that you are actually feeling is that imagining feeling a pain is having a sensuous representation that is qualitatively similar to the actual feeling of the pain but being less lively, so the representation will be superseded by the actual feeling. It follows from this that Prinz is right when he points out (2011a: 214; 2011b: 219) that empathy cannot be necessary for each and every moral attitude that we may adopt, e.g. the indignation that we may feel because of the pain that we are now suffering unjustifiably, or that an individual with whom we are hooked up is now suffering unjustifiably.

When you attribute the pain that you imagine to someone else, it is their pain that you will seek to relieve in the first instance. But if you cannot relieve the pain of the other, you may resort to relieving only the pain that you imagine and, thereby, the compassion that you feel. As Bloom mentions (2016: 74–5), if you empathize with the pain of somebody writhing in front of your eyes, and find that you can do nothing to remove the pain of this individual, you may resort to changing your location so that this individual is no longer within sight. For if you can no longer see this individual, your empathy is liable to subside and, thereby, your desire that the victim's pain be relieved, alongside the compassion and frustration that you will feel because this desire cannot be satisfied.

If the account of empathy given here is correct, is it possible to 'exploit people's empathy for good causes' (Bloom, 2016: 49), by trying to give it better direction? Such a strategy would seem preferable to the strategy of removing empathy that would risk leaving us motivationally dry and unconcerned about the weal and woe of our future selves and others. According to the present account, we are capable of modifying the direction of empathy because it is not only true that we *spontaneously or automatically* imagine having feelings that we believe others to undergo or ourselves to undergo in the future; we can also do this *voluntarily or at will*.[2] For instance, if we see a friend being cut, bleeding, screaming, grimacing and so on, we are likely to call to mind what it was like when we ourselves were cut, bled, etc., and the pain we then felt. This disposes us think that our friend is now feeling something like this pain. All this normally happens independently of our will, but our will can then take over and make us keep what we imagine in mind for some time. We are also capable of voluntarily obeying commands to imagine this or that.[3]

---

[2] This is a reason why it is important not to confuse empathy with emotional contagion: we cannot directly infect ourselves with emotions at will, though we can do so indirectly, e.g. by seeking the company of individuals who have the emotions with which we would like to be infected.

[3] Prinz claims: 'Imagination sounds like a kind of mental act that requires effort on the part of the imaginer' (2011a: 212). Yes, voluntarily imagining something could require effort, but it is quite frequently *not* imagining something that takes effort, if it is at all possible. For instance, I can barely bear watching the opening of Luis Buñuel and Salvador Dali's film *The Andalusian Dog* which shows a razor

Consider also a simple case involving only yourself: if you are told that you will probably feel acute pain later today, you will immediately be seriously concerned, think desperately about ways of escaping this pain, and feel fear that it cannot be avoided. This is because you automatically empathize with yourself later today, i.e. automatically imagine feeling the pain that you believe that you will be feeling shortly. By contrast, owing to the bias towards the near, your automatically imagining the acute pain that you hear that you might suffer next year will be much more fleeting and perfunctory, if it occurs at all. But your *reason* could inform you that your pain next year will one day be just as real and unbearable as your pain later today, and this may induce you to imagine *voluntarily* feeling next year's pain if this could help motivate you to find ways of avoiding it. If this voluntary piece of imagining is done with some persistence, it will most likely increase your sympathetic concern about feeling this pain, though it is unlikely to become as great as your concern about the pain later today, since the outcome of your act of voluntary imagination will probably be less vivid. True, a voluntary act of imagination presupposes that you are motivated to perform it, but the deliverance of your reason along with your automatic empathy, though perfunctory, may be enough to supply this amount of motivation which could inflate itself by means of a voluntary act of imagination.

Thus, we can counteract our bias towards the near with respect to our own well-being, though we are unlikely to overcome it completely. More often than we would like, it will continue to make us act in ways that we recognize as weak-willed and irrational. But although it would *now* often be better for us to be able to rise above this bias, it has probably served us well in the long past before the rational powers of our species developed to anything like the present level because the situations that it is most pressing to deal with are as a rule those in the nearer future.

---

cutting an eye, since I can't then help imagining feeling a razor cutting my own eye. I do not know how to prevent this piece of highly unpleasant imagining. Such automatic imagining is exceedingly common. The fact that our minds tends to pass automatically from one image to another if the second image represents a type of event that we have often observed succeeding the type of event that the first represents is famously exploited by Hume to explain our idea of a necessary connection between cause and effect (1739–40: I.iii.14).

Similarly, from an evolutionary point of view it is not hard to understand why our empathy with others is spontaneously selective. Spontaneously, we empathize strongly with individuals who we know well and with whom we have had mutually advantageous cooperation, like our kin and people in our community, but little, if at all, with strangers who might be treacherous and hostile for all we know. This makes evolutionary sense if sympathy and benevolent concern ride on the back of empathy because then we shall sympathize and be concerned about people in our own community and be comparatively unconcerned about outsiders, and this is likely to make our own community successful in the struggle for resources with outsiders.

But although we do not spontaneously empathize with some individuals for such reasons and, therefore, have little or no concern for them, our intellect could tell us that features that set some individuals apart from us, like a different colour of their skin, are not reasons to think that they suffer less than we do, or that their suffering merits less concern. They simply make it harder for us to empathize spontaneously with their suffering. So, we should make a voluntary effort to imagine as vividly the suffering of these strangers as we spontaneously imagine the suffering of those individuals more familiar to us. As a result, we might be filled with as much compassion for the suffering of the strangers as for those more familiar to us.

Consequently, by means of our power of reasoning, we can expand the range of our empathy, and thereby our sympathy and benevolent concern, to other individuals and further into the future, and make these attitudes less discriminatory. It should not be thought, however, that this process of moral enlightenment is easy for, as indicated at the end of 2.4, it may be that what makes our spontaneous empathy weaker for those who are observably different from us is in part the fact that our upbringing has conditioned us to denigrate them by attributing additional negative features to them. These denigrations may in themselves be quite incredible, but our conditioning has inclined us to shun evidence against them and seek evidence that confirms them because endorsement of them is a ticket to membership of important in-groups.

Further, even though we cannot strictly speaking empathize or sympathize with a greater number of individuals at the same time, we can with sufficient effort extend the motivational influence of our empathy to such groups by voluntarily imagining the suffering of a single individual in the groups, and reminding ourselves that the suffering of each individual in the groups is as real and unjustified as is the suffering of this individual and that the total suffering of the entire groups is as great as the suffering of all their members together. This will lead to our benevolence being channelled into actions designed to benefit the entire groups in so far as we can find such actions. But since it will generally cost us more to execute such actions than actions that would benefit fewer as much, we shall be less motivated to execute them. Thus, in order to make our benevolence towards a multitude effective, we need to raise our empathy to a high pitch by a strenuous multiplication procedure, which seldom could make up for what is beyond sensuous representation.

In sum, with the help of our reason we can counteract the fact that our empathy by nature is spatio-temporally biased, unjustifiably discriminatory, and innumerate, and voluntarily develop a more reflective empathy, though we would be hard put to overcome completely these shortcomings of our spontaneous empathy. Such a voluntary, reflective empathy would motivate a correspondingly more reflective and justifiable altruistic concern, as well as a greater, more rational prudential concern for our future selves. In other words, we are capable of a sort of motivational bootstrapping: we find ourselves concerned about others and ourselves in the near future because we automatically empathize with these individuals to some degree, and this concern could motivate us to reflect on the unjustifiability of possible grounds that tend to eclipse our automatic empathy for other individuals and ourselves in the more distant future, and to modify our concern for them in ways that we see as rationally justified by voluntarily imagining more lively what it is like to be them.

By this procedure we could surmount obstacles that evolutionary programming has put in the path of our empathy and benevolent concern. This is clearly a superior strategy to trying to divest ourselves of empathy because it is misdirected or restrictive, and thereby risk divesting ourselves of benevolent concern both for others and ourselves. It would certainly be a poor strategy to give up empathizing with our possible suffering in the distant future, say, from lung cancer from smoking cigarettes. Rather, we should develop a more reflective empathy which extends further into our future, by heeding our reason's advice to imagine more distant suffering as vividly as we spontaneously imagine suffering that is closer in time. This strategy is more likely to generate motivation to give up smoking now than is refraining from such a voluntary direction of imagination.

However, we have seen that there are features that do not merely block empathy and sympathy, but counteract them by giving rise to desires to harm others, even though this would not satisfy any self-interested desires of ours. These desires are of two kinds: malevolent desires towards individuals simply because they are disliked, and desires to harm them because this is thought to be deserved or just. In 2.3 I argued that our sense of justice could make us crack down on those who cheat us, for instance, by excluding them from beneficial cooperation. Our sense of justice manifests itself not only in our making judgements about what is (un)just, but also in our being motivated to some extent to rectify what we judge to be unjust. It is controversial what justice consists in, e.g. whether the notions of desert and rights are applicable, but we are motivated to do whatever we take it to consist in, though our motivation to do what we regard as just is likely to be weaker than our motivation to benefit those for whom we care most and to harm those who have aroused the most intense malevolence.

As remarked in 1.4, like many other animals, we practise the tit-for-tat strategy which consists in responding in the same coin, more specifically, being angry at and inclined to punish those who harm us or those close to us, and being grateful and inclined to reward those who benefit us or those close to us. From an evolutionary point of view, it is not hard to comprehend why we abide by this strategy. But in contrast to (most) other animals, we have the power to contemplate whether our spontaneous angry or grateful reactions are justifiable. The upshot of this contemplation may be that an angry and punitive response is seen to be unjust or unjustifiable because, say, the harm inflicted on us was accidental or unavoidable, or was inflicted in order to protect somebody else from much greater harm. So, reason may command us to hold back our spontaneous angry and punitive responses. We may, however, fail to comply with this command if we empathize strongly with the victims of harmful acts but not at all with their perpetrators. Such biased empathy might also get in the way of our making judgements about what is justifiable. We might be so incensed by the fact that we have been harmed that we ignore that the infliction of the harm was unavoidable or justifiable, and are carried away by malevolent desires.

Although Bloom concedes that 'empathy can serve as the brakes' on aggression and violence, he argues that 'it's just as often the *gas*' (2016: 188): 'the empathy one feels toward an individual can fuel anger toward those who are cruel to that individual' (2016: 208). But it is not empathy with the victim of cruelty that *triggers* the aggression towards the offender; it is our adherence to the tit-for-tat strategy that *moves* us to punish agents who are cruel to those we care about. Certainly, if we empathize with victims—but not with their aggressors—this tends to *amplify* our aggression, but it is not empathy that *makes* us angry at aggressors. If it is claimed that it is such an amplification of anger beyond reason that is what makes empathy undesirable in this connection, it could be countered that it offers the compensating good of serving as a brake on our anger if we direct it at the aggressors. Surely, this is not what you expect of something that is properly characterized as 'a powerful force for war and atrocity' (Bloom, 2016: 9).

I have contended that the removal of empathy is not a recommendable remedy (were it feasible). Although our sense of justice by itself motivates us to do what we judge to be just, the risk is that this motivation will be so weak in many of us that we would do little to rectify instances of injustice. For when we attempt to punish offenders, or to extract compensation from them, we usually have to stick our necks out, and we are disinclined to do so for individuals for whom we do not care at all. Likewise, we would also be unlikely to incur costs in order to reward those who have acted justly. Benefiting beings who are unfairly worse off or in greater need than others when this is simply the result of bad luck and not of the wrong-doing of any moral agents is of course also costly. A better strategy than removal of empathy is surely to empathize with those at the receiving end of unfair acts and misfortunes. Additionally, we could try boosting the motivational power of reasons of justice by imagining ourselves in the roles of those who suffer unjustly (who may not be conscious of this fact). However, we should not forget that a certain amount of empathy for possible offenders may be called for as well.

The importance of empathy as a brake on unjustified aggression and violence may be even clearer in the case of psychopaths. Bloom's conclusion about them is: 'They do tend to be low in empathy. But there is no evidence that this lack of empathy is responsible for their bad behavior' (2016: 201). Here it is important to bear in mind that empathy has a function to fill not only with respect to our concern for others, but with respect to our concern for our own future welfare as well. Psychopaths are characteristically unconcerned not only about other individuals, but about their own long-term future (and past), too. Hence, their 'lack of realistic long-term goals', their 'impulsivity' and 'irresponsibility' (2016: 198); their being 'relatively indifferent to punishment' and 'unmoved by love withdrawal', mentioned by Prinz (2011a: 218; cf. 2011b: 222). Now suppose—as seems true—that psychopaths are also prone to aggression and excessive vanity. It is obvious that such people could easily be driven to crime and other immoral behaviour to gain short-term profits because neither concern for others nor fear of punishment and social condemnation will hold them back.

3.3 Further Objections to the Moral Importance of Empathy

It might be objected that in order to act out of benevolent concern, we evidently do not need to empathize on each and every occasion. For instance, we might grab a pedestrian to prevent him or her from stepping out in front of a bus, without having had time to do any empathizing. Granted, but this may be because we have acquired a *habit* of acting in such ways, since we have often in the past empathized, and sympathized, with people in similar circumstances and, thereby, have acquired a *standing* motivation to help them out. If we have regularly helped individuals in certain types of situations because we have empathized and sympathized with them then, if we recognize the present situation as being of one of these types, this may be sufficient to make us help individuals out, without empathizing and sympathizing, especially if the help is not costly to us—so-called low cost altruism. Thus, empathy and sympathy may be necessary to make us concerned enough about others to act to start with, without subsequently being necessary for acting out of concern on each and every occasion (cf. Schopenhauer, 1995: 150).

Here surfaces a difference between concern, on the one hand, and sympathy and compassion, on the other, for although we might say that our act expressed concern for the well-being of the pedestrian, we would scarcely say that we had time to feel compassion for the pedestrian. The emotions of sympathetic joy and compassion do seem to involve empathy on each and every occasion. But 'concern' denotes a disposition to have occurrent desires on specific occasions, and this disposition may be actualized and manifested in occurrent desires without the assistance of empathy.

In the situation at hand, we are, however, likely to experience some emotion, in particular fear, just like the pedestrian, but it is noteworthy that this is nevertheless not an instance of emotional contagion, since our fear is a fear that *another* individual might be hit by the bus and results in our reaching out for this individual, whereas the pedestrian's fear is a *self-centred* fear that rather results in flinching away from the bus. In cases of emotional contagion, such as the fear of a predator spreading over a herd, it is a self-centred fear that spreads through the herd, the fear that '*I* might be caught by the predator'. And as de Waal notes, the self-centred response that emotional contagion produces 'doesn't provide a good basis for altruism' (2010: 74).[4]

At this juncture, it is also important to draw attention to the fact, noted in 1.2, that there is a sense of being concerned about something which is not *benevolent* concern, i.e. concern about its well-being or welfare, and which does not involve empathy at all. This is a sense in which we can be concerned even about inanimate things, that is, be concerned that they are not destroyed or damaged. Thus, if you see that a precious vase is about to fall, you might fear that it will be destroyed and reach out to save it. The existence of such concern should make us careful about ascribing empathy to very young children and animals on the basis of their making attempts to help or console others in trouble. To deal with this possibility, de Waal introduces the term 'preconcern' which 'doesn't require imagining yourself in the other's situation' (2010: 96). All

---

[4] But de Waal seems to overlook the distinction between the two kinds of fear when he discusses the case of spectators' reaction to 'the fall of a circus acrobat' (2010: 66–7). This case is, however, complicated by the fact that the acrobat's *performance* is likely to cause spectators to mimic the acrobat's movements, and this may indeed be symptomatic of emotional contagion (or empathy for that matter).

the same, he argues that 'some large-brained animals may share the human capacity to put themselves into somebody else's shoes' (2010: 96), that is, to empathize and be benevolent.

In the case of the pedestrian, there are no competing interests. But when there is such competition, one party often claims our spontaneous concern at the expense of others, for instance, when we have to harm a stranger to help a friend. Then our voluntarily directed, reflective empathy should step in and adjudicate between the interests at play. Consequently, the fact that we have developed standing desires that enable us to do the right thing on many occasions does not mean that engaging in empathy has been rendered redundant. Sooner or later spontaneous, selective empathy will assert itself, and the combat against its distortions must be resumed.

Sometimes our disposition to aid is held back by beliefs that we would scrap were we conscious of the fact that we hold them. Consider the so-called *bystander effect*, the fact that we are less likely to help someone in apparent need if we are surrounded by people who show no sign of helping. It might be that in these situations our disposition to help is kept in check by a belief that the other bystanders might know that help is not really needed and that we would make fools of ourselves were we to make attempts to help. If we realize this, we might conclude that it is worse risking to ignore somebody's need of aid than to risk embarrassing ourselves and, as a consequence, stage an attempt to aid.

Prinz relates studies showing that people who found a dime in a phone booth are much more likely to help a passer-by who has dropped some papers than people who did not find a dime. He concludes that a 'small dose of happiness seems to promote considerable altruism' (2011a: 220). Certainly, a standing disposition to be of assistance is more likely to manifest itself if we are happy than if we are depressed or angry. When we feel that things are going well for ourselves, we are more bent on empathizing with and making efforts to assist those who are less fortunate than we are if things are going badly for ourselves. If we are troubled, this is more likely to cause us to have emotions like envy and *schadenfreude*, or simply to remain indifferent if we are deeply depressed.

In any case, engaging in empathy is not necessary on each and every occasion for having altruistic or benevolent desires. The claim is rather that it is necessary for them to originate in the first place and an effective means of giving them a boost. Prinz thinks, contrariwise, that empathy could reduce the inclination to help because the 'vicarious distress' that he sees empathy as involving 'presumably has a negative correlation with positive happiness' (2011a: 220). But, to begin with, 'positive happiness' by itself does not seem to give rise to any inclination to help; happy people might consistently turn a blind eye to any misery that threatens to disturb their happiness. Furthermore, it should be remembered that empathy with the distressed does not involve actually *feeling* distress, but only *imagining* feeling the distress that others are believed to be feeling, which is less of a negative experience. Moreover, if we can help the distressed, we may end up actually feeling satisfied.

It should be stressed, however, that empathy is not an end in itself; it is emphatically not the case that the more we empathize, the better. Voluntarily empathizing is a *means* of boosting motivation to assist those in need, to enhance benevolent concern for them. But, as Bloom points out (2016: 133–46), people can empathize too much, so much that it can be harmful both to themselves and to those in need of their help. It can 'burn out' empathizers, making them depressed and emotionally exhausted. This is not surprising: after all, imagining feeling suffering is an unpleasant experience in itself, though not as unpleasant as actually feeling the suffering imagined. And it is not hard to understand how, say, doctors who are absorbed by acts of imagining the suffering of their patients might be overwhelmed and paralysed by what they imagine and be rendered unable to help their patients effectively.

But conceding that empathy can be excessive, that there can be too much of it, is not conceding that it is redundant, that there cannot be too little of it. In moderate measures it may be an efficient means of enhancing flagging compassion and benevolence. A Buddhist scholar quoted by Bloom states the appropriate recipe thus: 'meditation-based training enables practitioners to move *quickly* from feeling the distress of others to acting with compassion to alleviate it' (2016: 141, emphasis added).[5] Sometimes Bloom himself says essentially the

---

[5] For a survey of the ancient Buddhist tradition of cultivating empathy, see McRae (2017). In this tradition, 'empathy as imaginative projection' 'is assumed to be highly trainable', 'vastly under-utilized' (2017: 124), and also that it 'will

same: 'we know that feeling empathy for another makes you more likely to help them', though 'too much empathy can be paralyzing' (2016: 155–6).

However, even if we do not get caught up in excessive empathy, but use it wisely to quicken our sympathy and benevolent concern, it should be admitted that we run the risk of being burnt out: for those who are greatly concerned to relieve suffering in a world so full of misery as the actual one, awareness of the fact that, even if they were to comply with a very demanding morality, they could at best relieve only a tiny fraction of the suffering in the world might well be devastating. But the fact that a state of mind is devastating does not prove that it cannot be the state of mind of a morally enlightened person who tries to live up to moral norms. For, as will be argued in Chapter 5, the fact that norms are so demanding that it takes the utmost effort to comply with them is no objection to their validity. In itself, the contentment of moral agents is not an objective of morality.

All in all, the picture of the basis of morality that has emerged is this. In 1.1 it was seen that Schopenhauer construed this basis, compassion, as taking two forms: loving-kindness and justice. I have argued that instead of there being two forms of a single basic moral disposition, we have two independent kinds of basic moral dispositions: the empathy-based attitudes of compassion, along with sympathetic joy and benevolence, and a sense of or concern for justice (cf. Persson and Savulescu, 2012: 108; Persson, 2017). But I have stressed that these dispositions cannot function as reliable moral guides in their raw or spontaneous shape. For it has been seen that our spontaneous empathy is subject to various distortions, like the bias towards the near as opposed to the more remote future, the bias to those who are in various ways close to us as opposed to more distant, physically similar as opposed to dissimilar, and a numbness to numbers. Rational reflection tells us that these are limitations of our capacity for empathy which have nothing to do with the amount of well-being that the objects of empathy experience. Thus, we are rationally required to make voluntary efforts to rectify our empathy so that it mirrors this

---

stimulate compassion' (2017: 125)—precisely what has been argued here. See also Ricard (2015: pt. III).

well-being as accurately as possible. This will bring along a drastic expansion of our sympathy and benevolent concern for those who are more 'distant' from us in the various ways listed. On the other hand, we should be wary not to employ voluntary empathy excessively, so that it burns us out and gets in the way of acting out of benevolence.

There are also features that function as grounds for liking or disliking individuals rather than as filters on our capacity for empathy, such as their being friendly or hostile, physically or psychologically attractive or repellent. Although rationality requires us to consider to what extent it is just or justifiable to benefit or harm individuals in return for their having benefited or harmed us by these features, they sometimes occasion us to form benevolent or malevolent desires independently of consideration of this issue. It should also be kept in mind that the attribution of positive and negative features often serves to facilitate the attribution of further positive and negative features, respectively.

I have here conceived our sense of justice as a disposition to do what we *think* is just because I want to shelve the heated philosophical controversy concerning what justice really consists in, whether it is a matter of getting what we deserve, or something more egalitarian, etc. (but see Persson, 2017: chs. 7 and 8). This is another matter that would require rational scrutiny. But our desire to do what we think is just is comparatively weak and easily swayed by our empathy. It is therefore of vital importance for the cause of justice that the tendency of our empathy to partiality is kept in check.

Bloom writes that he has 'been arguing throughout this book that fair and moral and ultimately beneficial policies are best devised without empathy' (2016: 207). But even if it is true that such policies are best *devised* without empathy, I have contended that it is false that we can be best *motivated* to act in accordance with them without empathy. Consider again a simpler situation in the realm of prudence. If we have to devise a general policy for possible future circumstances in which we have to choose between a smaller, but still acute, pain the same day and a significantly bigger pain a week later, it is easy to tell what the best policy is: to opt for having the smaller pain the same day. The hard bit is to stick to this policy when the smaller pain will occur later today. In order to avoid backsliding, we then have to counteract our spontaneous empathy with ourselves in the imminent future by voluntarily imagining what it will be like for us to suffer the greater pain a week later. We shall most probably never succeed in voluntarily directing our empathy to the extent that we become temporally neutral and care as much about the more remote as the closer future. But it is still better to have an imperfectly reformed empathy than letting spontaneous empathy rule without resistance, or being without all empathy.

Bloom seems to concede something like this when speculating about how he would genetically engineer a child, he writes that he would be wary of removing empathy, but 'would ensure that it could be modified, shaped, directed, and overridden by rational deliberation' (2016: 212).[6] This could well be what has here been called voluntary, reflective empathy. Since he thinks that this child should be equipped with empathy, he must think that empathy is capable of doing some good. His case against empathy must then rest on it being impossible in fact to modify it to the extent that its existence is better than its non-existence.

In a similar vein, Prinz rejects the possibility 'to overcome the selective nature of empathy by devising a way to make us empathize with a broader range of people' (2011a: 228), because he thinks that empathy is 'intrinsically biased' (2011b: 229). To be sure, empathy probably cannot be modified to the degree that it will perfectly concord with the deliverances of rational deliberation, but it can be sufficiently reshaped that we are better off with it than without it, since in the latter case it seems that we would risk being totally unmotivated by any mental states beyond those of ourselves in the present.

In contrast to what I have argued, Michael Slote champions an 'ethics of care' which is 'avowedly partialistic in a way that utilitarianism and consequentialism...decidedly are not' (2007: 11). He maintains: 'Differences in (the strength of) normally or fully developed human empathy correspond pretty well to differences in intuitive moral evaluation' (2007: 16). Even if the latter claim is true, we should not assume that such an intuitive moral evaluation is necessarily correct. Although I believe that a moral principle of beneficence

---

[6] Cf. de Waal's remark: 'If I were God, I'd work on the reach of empathy' (2010: 204).

should be impartial or universal, like the utilitarian principle, it is not part of my present objective to give a full defence of this view, though arguing for the insignificance of our identity takes us quite a bit of the way. Apart from believing moral impartiality to be sound, it is a view I have here assumed because it is in tune with Schopenhauer's view. My objective has been to argue that, even though our empathy and the attitudes of sympathy and benevolence generated by it are spontaneously partial in various ways, this partiality can be rectified, so that it does not stand in the way of a moral principle of beneficence which is impartial.

As opposed to this, Slote argues, for instance, that the fact that we spontaneously empathize much more strongly with individuals before our eyes than with individuals known to us only by description justifies our having greater moral concern for them (2007: 2.1). I find this claim as implausible as a claim that our lesser spontaneous concern for suffering members of a crowd than for suffering individuals who present themselves to us one by one is justified. Or a claim that our lesser spontaneous concern for the suffering that will be inflicted on us in a couple of days than for our suffering later today is justified. It seems to me symptomatic that Slote takes the empathy to which he appeals to involve feelings how another feels that are elicited involuntarily, and to be a phenomenon that has a kinship with emotional contagion (2007: 13–14). As soon as we recognize that empathy instead consists in episodes of imagining that can be voluntarily controlled, spontaneous empathy will appear much less sacrosanct.

Slote ambitiously aims to show that 'a care-ethical approach makes sense across the whole range of normative moral and political issues' (2007: 1), issues such as deontology, justice, rights, and autonomy. His account of justice, however, does not address the point first made in 1.1 that a sense of justice could sharply conflict with empathy-based emotions. For instance, advocates of desert could desire that evil-doers be harshly punished, although this does not serve any good—as Kant's example of capital punishment might be taken to illustrate—simply because this is what justice requires. But this desire could be opposed by the tug of an empathy-based attitude of mercy—e.g. at the sight of how badly the evil-doers suffer—so that these advocates want to reduce the severity of the punishment that they insisted on inflicting at first.

In defence of the deontological act-omission doctrine, Slote maintains: 'Killing... does put us as agents in a shockingly closer connection to someone's harm than does allowing someone to die. It typically evokes a much more negative empathic response' (2007: 44). But we do not typically *empathize* more strongly, and feel more *compassion* for, someone in a burning building because we have caused rather than not caused the fire. As Slote points out, when we kill, 'we are in causal terms more strongly connected to a death than if we merely allow someone to die' (2007: 44). This stronger causal connection makes us feel more *responsible* for the ensuing death, and perhaps guilty and blameworthy, but this does not imply that our empathy for the victim increases.[7] For reasons such as these, it seems to me undeniable that a monistic care ethics such as Slote's faces insurmountable obstacles.

3.4 Morality and Self-Renunciation

Rationality and morality require us to widen dramatically the range of our spontaneous empathy and, thereby, our sympathy and altruistic concern, so that they better cover various out-groups, anonymous individuals, individuals in the distant future, non-human animals, and so forth. To implement such a widening is naturally an exceedingly demanding task, calling for great sacrifices of our welfare in order to benefit others. It should not be assumed, however, that such an extended altruism should necessarily take the maximizing form laid down by utilitarianism. For it is not obvious that in the domain of prudence we are rationally constrained to maximize what is good for ourselves over time,[8] and if personal identity is rationally insignificant, it might be asked why this constraint should then hold in the inter-personal sphere of morality, constraining us to maximize what is good for all over time. It is not part of my present aim to explore whether there might be ideals that could justify benefiting some individuals more than others. This is a topic I have pursued elsewhere (2005:

---

[7] See (2013: chs. 3 and 4), where I argue that the act-omission doctrine expresses a causally based sense of responsibility.

[8] As for instance Richard Hare contends in order to derive utilitarianism for the inter-personal sphere by means of the universalizability of intra-personal maximization (1981: pt. II).

pt. IV). In addition, it should be kept in mind that even if it were the case that our principle of beneficence ought to take a utilitarian format, our morality should not be utilitarian, since at least a principle of justice has to be acknowledged, as I have contended here and pursued at greater length in other work (e.g. 2005: pt. V and 2017: pt. II).

Whether or not rational self-concern requires an inter-temporal maximization of what is good for us, an adjustment to requirements of rationality will present a drastic and demanding challenge. Most of us acknowledge that rationality requires us to overcome the bias towards the near by imagining what might affect us for better or worse in the more distant future as lively as we spontaneously imagine our imminent future well-being. But as regards time, practical rationality requires us to take into account all temporal facts that might have a bearing on our attitudes. These facts include that our lives are played out in a temporally endless universe that will harbour events occurring billions of years after our death, many of which could be morally irrelevant because they could not feature any sentient beings.

It is not just an endless future that should be incorporated in the picture; there is evidently an endless past to fit in as well. With respect to it, there is another temporal bias that we must rise above, namely, *the bias towards the future*, which makes us spontaneously inclined to be much more concerned about our future than our past.[9] Defeating this bias requires us to regret as much worthwhile things in the past that we *have* missed as worthwhile things in the future that we *shall* miss. But if we imaginatively put our lives in a temporal perspective that stretches over events located both in an endless past and in an endless future, the significance of what happens at the present time shrinks almost to nothing owing to its being gauged in the framework of the mass of events that occur in the course of a temporally boundless universe.

It is further diminished if the *spatial* perspective is similarly broadened to comprise what occurs not just in our perceived neighbourhood, but also in the lives of trillions of other beings that are staged elsewhere in the universe. As mentioned in 2.3, we ordinarily exhibit a bias towards the perceived which makes us focus our

---

[9] Parfit discusses this bias in (1984: 165ff.), and I do so in (2005: ch. 16).

attention first and foremost on the minute section of the environment that our sense-organs pick up at the present time. Simultaneously, countless other events occur all across the universe of which we are oblivious. The satisfaction of your present desires will matter less to us if we view them in a framework of a longer stretch of our lives, and our lives will matter less to us if we view them in the framework of trillions of other lives, past, present, and future. Although we screen it out in everyday life, the fact is that we are in the midst of trillions of other creatures on earth who are just as engrossed by their current personal matters as we are. And the earth is just a vanishingly minute dot in a universe whose boundaries we cannot fathom.

As already the Stoic emperor Marcus Aurelius emphasized, when we look at ourselves from such a vantage-point 'far above' that surveys an overwhelming multitude of other beings, the importance of our preoccupations is drastically diminished (*Meditations*, 9. 30). The metaphor of 'far above' should, however, not mislead us into thinking that this perspective effaces finer details; instead, there should be a more extensive spatio-temporal coverage without any loss of finer details.

If we perform this feat of so to speak imaginatively transcending our particular position in space and time, an endless spatio-temporal vista opens up as a frame of reference for our concern. From such a viewpoint *sub specie aeternitatis*, as Spinoza put it, everyday states of affairs, however good or bad they may be for us, shrivel to insignificance. By contrast, when we zoom in on such states of affairs from an everyday, mundane personal perspective which does not range over much more than the near future and what is perceived by us, they could occupy a relatively large part of our frame of concern, since this perspective cannot contain sequences of events that are hugely more extensive in time and space. But with a shift to a cosmic perspective which ranges over more of the universe than the earth and over billions of years, a mind-bogglingly wide-ranging sequence of events becomes imaginable. Set in this framework, what we could accomplish in our transient lives dwindles to next to nothing, and accordingly our interest in it tends to be radically reduced.

Against the backdrop of the endless number of years ahead of us when we shall be dead, a few decades of welfare before we die shrink almost to nothing. Realizing how little difference our death will make to the state of the world corrects the excessive importance that we are lured to attach to our own role for the reason that we always perceive ourselves at the centre of things, around which everything revolves. Likewise, if we take pains to imagine in some detail the trillions of beings all around us striving for the satisfaction of their self-interested desires just like we do, we shall be loath to join their ranks with gusto.

Also, a more extensive temporal perspective reveals that when our desires have been satisfied, the sweet feeling of satisfaction will not last for long, even if it be the satisfaction of desires that have occupied most of our attention. It is likely to be replaced immediately by desires for something else, or else we are seized with boredom. Such a lively realization of the transience of fulfilment tends to sap the strength of our desires and release us from the treadmill of futile fulfilment-hunting. In contrast, if our time-frame does not reach much beyond the near future, we are disposed to be prodded by one desire after another in ignorance of how little their fulfilment has to offer us. If we compare being satisfied with being frustrated during a limited period of time, while being unaware of a much broader time-frame, being satisfied comes out as being supremely important for us. Consequently, we crave that the world supply us with more wealth, higher status, better health, and longer lives which could contain all this. But it is clear that this is an unsatisfiable craving, since however much we possess of these things, it is always possible to imagine having more.

With a switch from this mundane perspective to a point of view *sub specie aeternitatis*, which in addition encompasses trillions of other creatures, the fulfilment that we can possibly gain during the span of our lives, which from this point of view appears ephemeral, is by comparison reduced to something so petty that it is psychologically hard to get worked up about it. What we so earnestly chase comes out as flickering phantasms of tiny, short-lived organisms arbitrarily thrown out in a spatially and temporally boundless universe.

By reducing the strength of self-interested desires to promote exclusively our own well-being, the view from eternity joins forces with the consideration that somebody's being identical to ourselves is no reason for special concern. Taken together, they weaken the opposition that self-interest is capable of putting up against moral motivation like sympathy and altruistic concern, thereby making it easier for us to risk our own good in the line of doing what we morally

Morality and Self-Renunciation 97

ought. But the deliverances of the perspective *sub specie aeternitatis* are not wholly harmonious with morality, for they deflate our sympathy with and benevolent concern also for others for whom it is in our power to make things better, since they are virtually blotted out in a boundless spatio-temporal perspective in which it will eventually be as though they have never existed. However, since our self-concern, especially as regards the near future, is often inordinately strong, deflation will be most pronounced with respect to it. As a temptation is easier to keep in check if it is reduced in strength, this deflation will make self-concern easier to restrain, even though it retains its lead over other-regarding concern. Nonetheless, this goes to show that attitudinal compliance with what is seen from the point of view of eternity not only promotes moral motivation, but also counteracts it to some extent.

Schopenhauer, too, touches on the effects of a such-like perspective on us: 'If we lose ourselves in contemplation of the infinite greatness of the universe in space and time, meditate on the past millennia and on those to come... we feel ourselves reduced to nothing' (1966: I, 205). But his idealism has a remedy ready at hand: 'against such a ghost of our own nothingness... there arises the immediate consciousness that all these worlds exist only in our representation' (1966: I, 205). However, something like the adoption of a perspective *sub specie aeternitatis* makes a comeback in the shape of his idea of penetration of the *principium individuationis* of space-time to the reality behind. As mentioned, this act has an impact on our identity, since it cuts through the distinction between ourselves and others, so that a person will 'regard the sufferings of all that lives as his own, and thus take upon himself the pain of the whole world' (1966: I, 379). Such a person

> knows the whole, comprehends its inner nature, and finds it involved in a constant passing away, a vain striving, an inward conflict, and a continual suffering. Wherever he looks, he sees suffering humanity and the suffering animal world, and a world that passes away... that knowledge of the whole, of the inner nature of the thing-in-itself... becomes the *quieter* of all and every willing. The will now turns away from life; it shudders at the pleasures in which it recognizes the affirmation of life. Man attains to the state of voluntary renunciation, resignation, true composure, and complete will-lessness... it is no longer enough for him to love others like himself, and to do as much for them as for himself, but there arises in him a strong aversion to the inner nature whose expression is his own

phenomenon, to the will-to-live, the kernel and essence of that world recognized as full of misery...he ceases to will anything...tries to establish firmly in himself the greatest indifference to all things.
(1966: I, 379–80)

This process is described as a 'transition from virtue to *asceticism*' (1966: I, 380), in which one's own well-being is no longer sacrificed simply as a necessary means of alleviating the sufferings of others, but 'to serve as a constant mortification of the will, so that satisfaction of desires, the sweets of life, may not again stir the will' (1966: I, 381–2).

For Schopenhauer, 'moral virtues are a means of advancing self-renunciation, and accordingly of denying the will-to-live' (1966: II, 606). My suggestion has rather been that a tuning down of self-interest could serve as a means of clearing the way for moral motivation, though I do not think that it should be pursued primarily as such a means, but as something that is rationally required, required in order to internalize facts about our transience and the insignificance of our identity (as I argue more extensively in 2005). For Schopenhauer, there is, however, a moral dimension to self-renunciation, as we shall see. Another difference between us is that he speaks of a *denial* of the will, of a tuning down of willing to *zero* apparently, as a result of vividly taking on board the colossal amount of suffering that the world harbours, whereas for me it is more a matter of a 'dimming' of willing.

The source of this difference is in Schopenhauer's doctrine that feelings of pleasure, enjoyment etc. are nothing but the disappearance of negative feelings and that, therefore, the truth that 'it would be better for us not to exist' is 'the most important of all truths' (1966: II, 605).[10] Mine is the more commonsensical stance that life *could* be better for us than non-existence. If some of us lead good lives that are better for us than non-existence, we need not be altogether deluded in being hooked on the will to live because we could nourish some hope to be among the lucky number who are dealt lives worth living. But if we ascend to the view *sub specie aeternitatis* and gain a more compelling sense of the immense suffering of living creatures, our enthusiasm for life is muted, though not necessarily to the point of indifference.

---

[10] By contrast, Adam Smith took a very sanguine view: 'Take the whole earth at an average, for one man who suffers pain or misery, you will find twenty in prosperity and joy, or at least in tolerable circumstances' (1790: III.iii.8).

There is, however, an ambiguity in Schopenhauer's view. It would appear that the realization that all the suffering in the world in some sense belongs to oneself would give rise to a strong *aversion* to life, as indeed Schopenhauer himself puts it in the quotation above. One realizes that one cannot hope to draw a winning ticket, but rather as someone who 'takes all the tickets in a lottery must necessarily suffer a great loss' (1974: II, 316). This would create not merely an *absence* of a desire to live, but the presence of a desire not to live, a positive desire that there not be life. Such a desire seems to be a phenomenon that he rules out, however: 'what the will wills is always life', so 'it is immaterial and a mere pleonasm if, instead of saying simply "the will", we say "the will-to-live"' (1966: I, 275). If so, a will-not-to-live is a contradiction: a will-to-live-and-not-to-live. However, Schopenhauer also talks about 'will-lessness', of ceasing 'to will anything'. Perhaps his idea is that if the will can no longer will life, be a will-to-live, it must cease to will, i.e. cease to be, because willing not to live, being a contradiction, is impossible.

It would, however, seem more natural that will-lessness should be the upshot of a thought that what the world holds in store for us is neither pleasures nor pains, nothing either good or bad for us, or equal amounts of the good and the bad, rather than of a revelation that life is altogether suffering. But it might be that if someone were to 'take upon himself the pain of the whole world', he would be overcome by a crushing sense of his own powerlessness to decrease significantly the enormity of this suffering, and in despair be paralysed by an incapacity to will anything. Strictly speaking, this would be something of an over-reaction, for it is only if we cannot do *anything* to decrease the amount of worldly pain that the willing that manifests itself in intentional action to do something to reduce this pain is rendered impossible.

If the end of 'the transition from virtue to asceticism' amounts to will-lessness or a killing of all willing, it would appear to be a transition to something at odds with moral virtue, since it would extinguish a benevolent will to treat others well as an end in itself along with other instances of willing.[11] Although ascetics may be willing to make

---

[11] Cf. Shapshay (2019: 28). But Shapshay maintains that 'the only way strictly to live up to the "harm no one" part of the principle is to give up willing altogether through renunciation' (2019: 28). However, in 1.1 I suggested that the principle 'Harm no one; help everyone as much as you can' should be qualified. We are

greater self-sacrifices than those who are perfectly compassionate or benevolent, it is a mistake to represent asceticism as a more extreme form of the same disposition as all-encompassing benevolence, for there is more than a difference in degree between a will to make sacrifices as a means to benefit others and as a means to a mortification or 'breaking of the will' (1966: I, 392). It might be that the moral virtue of altruism could be 'a means of advancing self-renunciation' in the sense that the sacrifices that altruistic people have to make are a part of the sacrifices ascetics have to make, but the ultimate end of asceticism would still be incompatible with that of altruism. In Schopenhauer's own words, it is 'one's own woe', not 'another's weal' (1966: II, 607n).

It might, however, be thought that we have ended up in this conundrum because we have forgotten a distinction already alluded to. The will to be stamped out—or rather reduced to a minimum necessary to stay alive—is only the will in so far as it is *self-interested* or *self-regarding*. A desire of yours is self-interested or self-regarding just in case it is *ultimately* about *you* being affected, or contains an *ineliminable* reference to you being affected. For instance, your desire that you give money to a certain beggar is unlikely to be self-regarding, since it is likely to be derived from a desire that the beggar gets money, along with a premise to the effect that you are best positioned to give the beggar money. By contrast, your desire that you be happy is likely to be ultimately about your being affected (for the better), and not being derived from a desire for an end not having to do with you. The desire to give money to the beggar, however, is probably other-regarding, for even if it is derived from a desire which does not refer to this particular beggar, it will probably be about another individual

---

allowed to harm *ourselves*, both as a means to the renunciation of our will and as a means to the greater good of others. The reason is that this is harming to which we cannot reasonably object. Likewise, I proposed that we are also permitted to harm *others* if this is harming to which they could not reasonably object. Therefore, to have some measure of credibility, the first half of the imperative must be tantamount to something like 'Harm no one in ways to which they could reasonably object'. But it would be implausible to claim that living up to this injunction requires us 'to give up willing altogether'. This is especially so, since the injunction, thus understood, does not apply to non-human animals who are incapable of reasonable objecting.

than yourself being affected, e.g. the first needy person in sight being affected.[12]

The proposal would be that individuals in pursuit of the ascetic ideal should have self-regarding desires for suffering, since it is Schopenhauer's view that 'the more one suffers, the sooner is the true end of life [i.e. will-lessness] attained' (1966: II, 635), and only minimal self-regarding desires for the necessary goods of life, such as food and drink. As I shall now argue, these self-regarding desires can be combined with an other-regarding aversion to the suffering of others.

Shapshay, however, asks a question that needs to be answered (2019: 31): if ascetics should seek suffering in order to liberate themselves, how do they then know that the compassionate striving to mitigate the suffering of others will not be counter-productive by chaining these others to life and more suffering in the longer run? Well, they might not *know* this in particular cases but, given that personal suffering works to liberate very few of us, it is *highly unlikely* that it will do so for any particular individual. Moreover, on Schopenhauer's view, we are bound to come across more suffering later in life, so we shall not run out of chances to attain salvation by means of suffering.

Granting that this may be the case, it still seems that some actions that are commonly thought of as beneficial will have to be dropped from the compassionate agenda, for example, not being killed or having our lives saved when death would be unexpected, swift, and painless. But we can perhaps understand why this type of act should not be dropped if we turn to Schopenhauer's reason for denying that suicide is a way out of a world of suffering. His reason is that the suicide proceeds by 'destroying the will's phenomenon, the body, so that the will may remain unbroken' (1966: I, 399). The will has to be broken, but this can only be done by the *insight* that the will brings in its wake endless suffering. But what of people who commit suicide because they realize precisely this, that a continuation of willing leads

---

[12] The rejection of the view that the distinction between what is within the domain of morality and what is not coincides with the boundary between oneself and others implies that it is inaccurate to speak about self-regarding and other-regarding desires, but it is accurate enough for the actual world which contains no such phenomena as successors.

to a surplus of suffering? Perhaps Schopenhauer would reply that this motive will not do because it consists in affirming a self-interested desire to the effect that *the self* escapes future suffering through death.

It might, however, seem that even ascetics are in the grip of such a self-interested desire because they desire to suffer not for its own sake, but in order to break their will and by this means to avoid future suffering: they 'deliberately make their life as poor, hard, and cheerless as possible, because they have their true and ultimate welfare in view' (1966: II, 638). If so, their motive would ultimately be egoistic and not moral. We might, however, get an inkling of how Schopenhauer could try to reply to this problem if we turn to his account of why the end of Stoic morality does not 'betray a really ascetic tendency' (1966: II, 159). He explains that this is because it does not have 'a metaphysical tendency, a transcendent end, but an end that is wholly immanent and attainable in this life: the imperturbability...and unclouded serene happiness of the sage whom nothing can assail or disturb' (1966: II, 159). Here Schopenhauer seems to advance the idea that a necessary condition for a morality having an ascetic tendency is that it has a metaphysical tendency. Now his morality has such a tendency in virtue of setting up the goal of breaking our will by peeking through the veil of spatio-temporal differentiation; so, it could qualify as ascetic.

But what is supposed to happen metaphysically when the will is broken? How is this different from what happens to the will when the body is destroyed in death? If there is a difference, it would seem that when ascetics succeed in breaking their will, it cannot just be that their own individual will, in the sense of a particular objectification of the will, is annihilated, for this surely happens in bodily death as well. It might be thought that the difference is that only in the former case is the will *as thing-in-itself* reduced, so that there is less will left to objectify itself in future sufferers. This would be a possible moral objective, though as an effect on possible beings who are prevented from beginning to exist it goes beyond the reach of compassion, as remarked in 3.1. The breaking of one's will would then stand at the intersection of egoism and morality because this act would benefit not just oneself, but would make the world better overall by bringing down the number of future sufferers in which the will is objectified.

There is a hitch, however: Schopenhauer apparently rules out any *partial* reduction of the will as thing-in-itself: 'if any being even the smallest were completely annihilated, then in it and with it the whole world would have perished' (1974: II, 221; cf. 1966: I, 128–9). This is so because 'the will-to-life...exists whole and undivided in every being' (1974: II, 221). But surely he cannot mean that when a single ascetic succeeds in breaking (or taming) his or her self-interested will, the whole world comes to an end.

This puts me in the disappointing position of having no answer to what happens metaphysically when ascetics break their self-interested will, but it would seem that this must be something that is not beneficial solely for themselves. For he maintains that 'Stoic ethics' is 'not a doctrine of virtue, but merely a guide to the rational life, whose end and aim is happiness through peace of mind', and that virtue features in it only 'as a means, not as end' (1966: I, 86). Since he views 'moral virtue' as a means to asceticism, it seems that he must assume asceticism to be a virtue, presumably because its end is not merely one's own peace of mind, or freedom from suffering. If ascetics have less burdensome ways of decreasing their own suffering—e.g. suicide— then, if they choose more burdensome way of doing so—by a denial of their own self-interested will—because this does most to decrease the suffering of others, they could be morally virtuous. But I do not understand how a denial of the will could be what necessarily reduces the suffering of others most—more than simply compassionately benefiting others—if it does not mean that there is less will to go round for objectification in future sufferers, which implies that the will-in-itself can be partially reduced.

As has been seen, ascetics could continue to have other-regarding desires, despite the renunciation—or extensive reduction—of their self-interested desires. Even though their ascetic life-style may reduce their ability to assist others, they could go on striving to ameliorate the suffering of other humans, being reasonably confident in most cases that this will not be counter-productive, since most humans are not capable of using their suffering as a means to their salvation. If, against the odds, the spirit of self-renunciation should spread widely, would-be ascetics would have to cut down on their other-regarding desires and for the most part leave their fellow-humans alone in their endeavours to reach salvation by means of suffering. Eventually, we might reach a state in which no adults have any will at all (and there will be no children, since humans will have stopped reproducing themselves years ago). Then, Schopenhauer seems to think, *nothing at all* would exist: 'with the highest phenomenon of the will [the human], the weaker reflection of it, namely the animal world, would also be abolished' (1966: I, 380). The result will be: 'No will: no representation: no world... there is certainly left only nothing' (1966: I, 411).[13]

I have tried to outline an interpretation of Schopenhauer's view that 'moral virtues are not really the ultimate end, but only a step towards' an ascetic end of will-lessness which is not just beneficial for the ascetics themselves, but virtuous by benefiting others as well (1966: II, 608). It builds on a distinction between self-regarding and other-regarding desires. If individuals on the path to self-renunciation prioritize the fulfilment of their other-regarding desires at the expense of fulfilling their self-regarding desires, this could serve the function of minimizing the fulfilment of the latter. They could be successful in this enterprise, even though they keep undiminished other-regarding desires concerned with reducing the suffering of others partly for its own sake only as long as they can confidently believe that others are incapable of using their suffering effectively as a means to self-renunciation. If this minimizing of fulfilment of self-regarding desires leads to a breaking of the will, this means a further reduction of suffering, one's own as well as the suffering of others.[14]

But this account relies on elements of Schopenhauer's view that remain shrouded in mystery, namely, a notion of a partial reduction of

---

[13] If there are aspects of the thing-in-itself that are not captured by the characterization of it as will—a possibility that Schopenhauer toys with, as indicated in 2.3—it could 'remain as the inner nature of the thing-in-itself, when this... has freely abolished itself as *will*' (1966: II, 198). In 2.3 it was also remarked that he entertains a notion of consciousness without object that could accompany this remnant. Perhaps his vacillation about whether there is absolutely nothing left is due to the fact that he thinks that 'our inner nature revolts' (1966: II, 199) against the idea of annihilation.

[14] Shapshay (2019: ch. 2) opposes the standard interpretation of Schopenhauer, according to which the end of all-encompassing compassion is subordinate to the end of the renunciation of the will, and a mere means or step towards it. But on the present account which draws on a distinction between self-regarding and other-regarding desires, there is no '*fundamental conflict*' (2019: 32) between compassion and self-renunciation, as she asserts. If there were a conflict, I doubt that Shapshay would be right that '*even on Schopenhauerian grounds we should prefer the ideal of compassion to that of resignationism*' (2019: 34). This view contradicts his explicit claim that 'moral virtues are a means of advancing self-renunciation'.

an indivisible will. Apart from this apparent contradiction, it was seen in 2.3 that there are several difficulties with the idea of sentient beings being objectifications of a will. Furthermore, if all adult humans were to break their wills, could this plausibly be thought to result in the will as thing-in-itself and, thus, the whole world, being annihilated? He held that 'theoretical egoism'—the doctrine that only the self and its representations exist—as 'a serious conviction' 'could be found only in a madhouse' (1966: I, 104), but it might be wondered whether his move of postulating a will of which representations are objectifications does much to raise credibility. The existence of the universe is still dependent on the existence of something psychological: not that your consciousness is not snuffed, but that your will is not broken.[15]

A further feature compounds the mystery surrounding the denial of the will, as understood by Schopenhauer. This is that it 'is not to be forcibly arrived at by intention or design, but comes... suddenly, as if flying in from without' (1966: I, 404). It 'arises from the direct encroachment of the freedom of the will-in-itself, knowing no necessity, on the necessity of its phenomenon' (1966: I, 403). Thus, the will-in-itself is thought to deny itself freely. This '*self-suppression of the will* comes from knowledge' (1966: I, 404), but how is this possible when 'originally and by its nature, knowledge is completely the servant of the will' (1966: I, 176)? Schopenhauer answers this question by distinguishing between the will's 'knowledge of its own inner nature' and the 'different kind of knowledge, whose objects are only phenomena' (1966: I, 404). Only the first kind of knowledge can be a 'quieter' of the will, so that knowledge passes 'into an activity not stimulated by the will, and therefore no longer serving it' (1966: II, 206).

In 2.4 we have, however, seen reasons to doubt that knowledge of the inner nature of the will could be principally different from knowledge of phenomena: it, too, must have a subject-object form and, since the will is inseparable from its objectification in the body, the form of space as well as time. But even if it had been crucially different, it might seem that, being knowledge, it must still be a servant of the will. For my own part, I believe that the view that knowledge and

---

[15] D. W. Hamlyn, for one, concurs that Schopenhauer's doctrine of salvation is 'an exceptionally difficult one' and 'it is far from clear what actual or real understanding of it is available' (1980: 149).

cognition are generally subservient to the will is false. They can derive from perception and inference which are independent of the will, and could then influence the will. Schopenhauer holds, to boot, a rather extreme version of the subservience of the will: 'the intellect remains so much excluded from the real resolutions and secret decisions of its own will that sometimes... it must surprise the will in the act of expressing itself' (1966: II, 209). The contrary view that the intellect may on occasion influence our will underlies my account of voluntary and reflective empathy in the preceding sections. As indicated there, this is a position enshrined in Buddhism, so despite his general admiration for this religion, Schopenhauer diverges from it in this respect. However, a discussion of his theory of freedom of the will, with its reference to the stumbling-block of his notion of the will-in-itself, would bring us too far afield to be pursued here.

4
Biases in Favour of the Negative

4.1 Negativity Biases and Negatively Weighted Utilitarianism

In 1.2 Schopenhauer was quoted as claiming:

> pain, suffering that includes all want, privation, need, in fact every wish or desire, is *that which is positive and directly felt and experienced*. On the other hand, the nature of satisfaction, enjoyment, and happiness consists solely in the removal of a privation, the stilling of a pain; and so these have a *negative* effect. Therefore, need and desire are the condition of every pleasure or enjoyment. (1995: 146)

This is his official view, the one that he often states explicitly, but he sometimes expresses himself as though positive feelings are feelings in their own right. For example, he describes 'immoderate joy or pain' as 'two excessive strains of the mind' (1966: I, 317). It is decidedly odd to call joy a 'strain' if it is merely a disappearance of a feeling, and such a disappearance could hardly be 'immoderate' or 'excessive'. He continues: when the delusion which occasions immoderate joy 'vanishes, we must pay for it with pains just as bitter as the joy caused by its entry was keen' (1966: I, 318). Here it certainly sounds as though he was comparing the intensity of two feelings and finding them equal. Nevertheless, on the very next page, he restates his official view: 'All satisfaction, or what is commonly called happiness, is really and essentially always *negative* only, and never positive' (1966: I, 319). Thus, I regard all indications to the contrary as mere slips,[1] a common

---

[1] Except when in 'Aphorisms on the Wisdom of Life' he sets himself the task of outlining an 'eudaimonology' or 'instructions on how to have a happy existence';

enough phenomenon among philosophers who champion some counter-intuitive doctrine.

Granted, sensations of pleasure are often preceded by sensations of painful tensions or the like. For instance, if, by stretching our legs, we eliminate the pain that we have been feeling because we have been sitting in a cramped position, a pain may give way to a pleasure. But even here the pleasure would evidently be a sensation in its own right, not just the disappearance of the pain, which would result if our legs simply became numb. However, it seems that Schopenhauer sometimes slides fallaciously from the claim that a positive feeling never 'comes to us originally and of itself, but it must always be the satisfaction of a wish'—a wish presumably being thought to be felt as something negative—to the claim that it 'can never *be* more than deliverance from a pain, from a want' (1966: I, 319, my emphasis). But we cannot infer what something is in itself from what it originates from.

Furthermore, in some situations in which we feel pleasure—e.g. when we unexpectedly taste or smell something good—this feeling does not follow on the heels of any painful or unpleasant sensation. Nor is it felt as pleasant because we antecedently wished to have such a sensation. True, when we are feeling the pleasant sensation, we like it, or want it to continue, but we want this because the sensation is pleasant; it is not pleasant because we want it to continue.[2] Still, it may be that pleasure which is preceded by negative sensations of tension, irritation, need, and so on, is usually more intense than pleasure which is not.

The example of a pleasurable taste or smell is also a reminder that sometimes physical pleasure is the opposite not of pain but of *disgust*; for instance, it is not painful but disgusting to taste or smell something rotten.[3] Disgust can be more intense than pleasure and make us vomit violently. Pain can likewise be more intense than pleasure. It is symptomatic that nobody has been crazy enough to uphold the view that

---

then he *consciously* abandons 'the higher metaphysical ethical standpoint to which my real philosophy leads' (1974: I, 311) for the time being.

[2] I discuss pleasure at greater length in (2005: ch. 2).

[3] It is noteworthy that there is a wider array of unpleasant than pleasant sensations: not only pain and disgust, but itches, dizziness, sensations of thirst and hunger, dazzling light, deafening sound, etc. See Persson (2005: ch. 1).

pain or disgust is just the absence or cessation of pleasure, a neutral state. Pain and disgust can simply be so intense that their existence is undeniable; for example, nobody could seriously assert that being exposed to the most painful torture is on a par with being unconscious!

This psychological asymmetry with respect to intensity between positive and negative feelings might lead us to exhibit what might be called *a general moral negativity bias*. It is commonly agreed that having negative experiences like the suffering that results from having painful sensations that we dislike for their own sakes are intrinsically bad for us, and that having positive experiences like the enjoyment that results from having pleasant sensations that we like for their own sakes are intrinsically good for us. Assuming this to be so, the upshot could be a general moral negativity bias to the effect there is *in general* more of a moral reason to reduce—that is, to remove, prevent, or avoid producing—what is intrinsically bad for individuals than to increase what is intrinsically good for them because the former benefits them more. It benefits them more because the reduction of the greater intrinsic badness of e.g. pain is likely to be tantamount to a greater boost of their welfare level than the increase of the intrinsic goodness of pleasure. More precisely, increasing goodness should here be understood as increasing goodness *directly*, as opposed to doing it by reducing what is intrinsically bad, e.g. cramp in the legs; otherwise, there would be an overlap with reduction of what is intrinsically bad.

Such a general moral negativity bias is something that traditional utilitarians could consistently accept. By contrast, there might be a *strict* moral negativity bias that they could not consistently accept. The strict bias is the intuition that there is more of a moral reason to reduce what is intrinsically bad for individuals than to increase *to an equal extent* what is intrinsically good for them. This bias supports what might be termed a *negatively weighted utilitarianism, nw-utilitarianism*, which declares that there is *stronger* moral reason to reduce what is bad for individuals than to increase (directly) what is good for them to an equal degree, so that what is good for individuals has a smaller moral weight than what is equally bad for them. If sound, the strict moral negativity bias would support this view, but it will here be argued this bias is not sound.

Nw-utilitarianism is a less extreme and more plausible version of a *negative utilitarianism* to the effect that there is *only* moral reason to reduce what is bad for individuals as much as possible, and *no* moral reason to increase what is good for them; in other words, that only what is bad for individuals has moral weight. Karl Popper may have expressed something like this when he wrote: 'Instead of the greatest happiness for the greatest number, one should demand, more modestly, the least amount of avoidable suffering for all'.[4]

We could compare a brief instance of suffering owing to physical pain, with an equally brief instance of enjoyment or happiness owing to physical pleasure, and judge them to be equally intense. Speaking of such suffering and happiness of 'equal intensity', Jamie Mayerfeld maintains that 'the intense suffering would not be compensated by an episode of the intense happiness lasting for a considerably *longer* amount of time' (1999: 133) This is explicitly a claim he makes about a *moral* asymmetry between suffering and happiness, though it is a claim about the intra-personal domain, since the suffering and happiness are supposed to be experienced by the same individual. Consequently, it expresses a strict moral negativity bias.

It might be thought that G. E. Moore also embraced this bias when he claimed that 'the mere consciousness of pleasure, however intense, does not *by itself*, appear to be a *great good*', whereas 'consciousness of intense pain...*by itself* may be a great evil', even if there is not 'an emotion directed towards' it (1903: 212). But to clarify what Moore's view might be, we need to keep in mind the distinction between pleasure being good (and pain being bad) *for the individuals who feel it*—it being *relationally* or *relatively* good (bad)—and it being *morally* good (bad), i.e. there being a moral reason to promote pleasure (prevent pain), *whoever might feel it*. His view might then seem to be that, whereas pain would be bad for us even if we have no dislike 'directed towards' it, pleasure would not be good for us if we do not like it. But this is implausible; surely, the more plausible view is that just as pleasure is relatively good for us (in itself) only in so far as we like it (in itself), pain is relatively bad for us (in itself) only in so far as we dislike it (in itself); and that it is only when these attitudes of liking and disliking are present that there is a moral reason to promote our

---

[4] Popper adds the egalitarian demand that 'unavoidable suffering...should be distributed as equally as possible' (1966: ch. 9, endnote 2).

pleasure and prevent our pain. I shall proceed on the assumption that it is such liked pleasures and disliked pains with which we are dealing. The question is then whether there is more of a moral reason to prevent pains than to produce pleasures that are as (intrinsically) good for the individuals who feel them as the pains are (intrinsically) bad for them.

The view that the negative moral value of pain is greater than the positive moral value of pleasure of the same intensity and duration—so that the pleasure is as much liked and relatively good for the subject as the pain is disliked and relatively bad—could take different forms. In its simplest form, the greater negative moral value of pain tracks changes in intensity and duration of sensations in the same way as the positive moral value of the counterpart pleasure does. So, for instance, considering sensations of the same intensity and duration, increases of the intensity of a pleasure raise its positive moral value as much as the same increases of the intensity of pain raise its negative moral value, so that the proportionate degree to which the negative moral value is greater remains constant.

However, Thomas Hurka develops a more sophisticated type of theory, according to which the negative moral value of pain increases at a greater rate the higher the intensity of pain, whereas with respect to the positive moral value of pleasures, the rate instead diminishes with higher intensities.[5] But it would be premature to pursue such more sophisticated views as long as we have not settled whether negative experiences have *any* greater moral weight than corresponding positive experiences.

Returning to Mayerfeld, he affirms that there is a moral asymmetry between suffering and happiness even in the intra-personal case; so it apparently follows that we could be acting *morally* wrongly if we intentionally suffer a pain in order to enjoy an equally intense pleasure that lasts longer. As should be evident from Chapter 2, I think that his claim should have been that we then make a *prudential* rather than a moral mistake, since dealing with what is good and bad for nobody but

---

[5] (2010: 203–6). Hurka claims this form to be a version of prioritarianism, but it does not imply, for example, that we should rather cause pain to somebody who feels only pleasure than somebody who has only neutral experiences, whereas prioritarianism would be expected to do so.

ourselves is a prudential instead of a moral matter. *Others* could be making a moral mistake were they to guide us to have the longer pleasure along with the shorter pain because they would be dealing with what is good and bad for somebody else. But I seriously doubt that they would regard such guidance as mistaken. If this is right, it indicates that we are not attracted to the strict negativity bias in intra-personal cases.

On the other hand, there is evidence for the operation of a strict moral negativity bias in *inter-personal* cases, for that there can intuitively be more of a moral reason to prevent the pain of somebody who is better off than to let somebody else who is worse off feel a pleasure of the same magnitude (i.e. of the same intensity and duration), even though the latter would do more to put these subjects on the same welfare level. Compare a choice between either preventing a rather severe pain of somebody who is better off or causing somebody who is worse off to feel a pleasure of the same magnitude, which would do more to put the two individuals on the same welfare level. We can imagine that this could be accomplished by giving either of them a pill which would neutralize the pain that the first individual is about to have or induce pleasure in the second individual. While familiar distributive doctrines like prioritarianism and egalitarianism would support producing the pleasure, nw-utilitarianism would recommend preventing the pain, which may seem intuitively plausible. Utilitarianism would be indifferent between these alternatives.

Notice that this example is about *preventing* pain (owing to causes other than our own agency) rather than *causing* it because, according to common sense, there certainly is an asymmetry between *negative rights* not to be interfered with in harmful ways that others have against us and *positive rights* to be benefited that they have, to the effect that the former are clearly stronger. Thus, our intuition that it would be wrong to cause one individual pain along with as much pleasure to another individual rather than causing neither could be due to the fact that the former involves an act that violates a more stringent right than the latter discharges. If so, it does not show that pain has a greater moral weight than the same amount of pleasure. The greater stringency of negative rights can be brought out by considering that it could be impermissible to take, e.g. food from someone who has a right to it and give it to someone else who does not have a right to it, though it would relieve the pangs of hunger of the latter more than it would relieve those of the former.

So, we must take care to exclude the influence of the stronger reasons against violating negative rights. It should be noticed that our reason not to violate negative rights by our own actions is considerably stronger also than our reason against *letting* such rights be violated by the actions of others. In other words, our responsibility for actively violating negative rights is greater than our responsibility for allowing them to be violated by others (and even by ourselves in the future). Therefore, our reason not to let someone else take the food from someone who has a right to it and give it to someone else who needs it more is weaker than our reason against doing this ourselves. This is implied by what is often called the act-omission doctrine, which like the doctrine of negative rights is enshrined in common-sense morality.[6]

In the case of the pill, both of these distorting factors are eliminated if it is stipulated that neither of the individuals involved has more of a right to be given the pill than the other and that we are acting as much if we give the pill to the one as to the other. Consequently, if, as may appear plausible, we have more of a reason to prevent the pain than to produce the pleasure, it seems that this must be the result of the differing moral weight of these experiences.

As was noted earlier, the elimination or mitigation of pain could also have the effect of producing pleasure. This means that we may not compare like with like if we consider choices between either eliminating an existing pain of one individual or producing an equal pleasure of another. For the former option will in fact benefit the recipient more if the elimination of pain generates some pleasure. This distorting factor is hopefully ruled out by framing the case in terms of preventing a pain from beginning which will not occasion any pleasure if the subject is unaware of the prevention.

It is not merely, as Mayerfeld suggests at one point (1999: 150–1), that this asymmetry between the positive and the negative is *steeper* across lives than within lives. It seems to me that there is *no* prudential

---

[6] I discuss the relation between the doctrine of negative rights and the act-omission doctrine further in (2013: ch. 3).

(or moral) asymmetry within lives, *no* prudential (or moral) objection to undergoing oneself, or letting somebody else choose to undergo, a pain in order for them to experience an equally great pleasure (in terms of intensity and duration), let alone a greater pleasure.

The question is, then, what could explain such a discrepancy between inter-personal and intra-personal cases. But, to complicate matters further, it may be that it is not always the case that we are inclined to relieve someone's pain rather than to let another have an equal pleasure. For suppose that one individual, Lesslie, is worse off than Bestie because Lesslie earlier suffered as much pain as now threatens Bestie, as a means of Bestie receiving as much pleasure as Lesslie will now receive as a result of Bestie's pain. Then it may no longer seem wrong to let Lesslie have the pleasure at the expense of Bestie getting pain. Thus, when the pleasure and pain to be distributed have precise counterparts in pleasures and pains earlier distributed to the same recipients, we may be prepared to let the pleasure occur at the price of pain, since this enables the recipients 'to get even'. But our moral negativity bias manifests itself at least in that we are not always prepared to accept such distributions even when they would decrease the difference between the better-off and the worse-off.

It is, however, hard to see how we could justifiably abide by the standard utilitarian view that the moral and prudential values of both pleasure and pain correspond to the relational value that they have for their subjects in virtue of their duration and intensity in intra-personal cases, but reject this view for inter-personal cases. A possible way out would be to suggest that we are not really prepared to commit ourselves to the strict bias and to contradict the standard utilitarian view. The suggestion might be that our habit of following the *general* negativity bias is so firm that unawares we remain under its influence even in cases in which it is only the *strict* bias that is applicable. We are so accustomed to thinking that we have more of a moral reason to reduce negative experiences involving pain than to increase positive experiences involving pleasure because the reduction of the negative will usually be greater than the increase of the positive that we forget what justifies this habit, and slip into thinking that we have more of moral reason to reduce negative experiences than to increase positive experiences even when the reduction will not be greater than the increase.

We should expect that pains (and the attendant suffering) can be more intense than pleasures (and the attendant enjoyment) because pains are generally signs of something that is injurious to our bodies and could damage them *irreversibly*. The *enhanced* bodily well-functioning that pleasure signifies is not irreversible and, so, is not likely to bring comparable gains. The *ordinary* state of good health is not accompanied by any pleasure at all.[7] Thus, it is to be expected that pains can be more intense than pleasures because, generally, they are signs of things more important for our reproductive fitness. The bodily conditions that produce pain may result in bodily injuries that permanently reduce our capacity to benefit from life and, thereby, irrevocably put these benefits out of our reach; if the worst comes to the worst, they may even result in death, and the loss of *all* the benefits of life forever. Therefore, the extrinsic badness of these conditions is great. So, it is important that they be removed as quickly as possible, and they may be removed if the pains that they occasion are eliminated or alleviated.

Pleasures are usually caused by conditions that are beneficial to our organisms and enhance our capacity to benefit from life. This enhancement is thus extrinsically good for us, and it is desirable that it be promoted, but this extrinsic goodness is generally smaller than the extrinsic badness of the harmful conditions. For while the loss of capacities is often irreversible when it is occasioned by damage to bodily organs, the acquisition of capacities is never permanent. Capacities often need to be kept up by practice and use, and even if they are, they will eventually be lost by increasing age and death.

In a similar vein, David Benatar notes that 'we must continually work at keeping suffering (including tedium) at bay, and we can do so only imperfectly' (2006: 77). We must make efforts to obtain the pleasures of drinking and eating and of having comfortable places to rest. The pains and unpleasant sensations of thirst, hunger, and being uncomfortable come naturally if we do not do anything, and with continuing passivity they tend to become unbearable, as the physical conditions causing them threaten our health or existence. By contrast,

---

[7] Perhaps it is such facts that are on Schopenhauer's mind when he argues 'if life... had positive value and in itself real intrinsic worth, there could not possibly be any boredom' (1974: II, 287).

we have to have a certain psycho-physical 'equipment' to lead a life better than non-existence. We must perform various more or less exerting actions to maintain—not to mention enhance—this equipment. If we fail to perform these actions, we lose more or less of this equipment, and some losses may be irreversible.

Secondly, while loss of capacities *excludes* benefits that could accrue from exercising the capacities, acquisition of capacities does not by itself *guarantee* such benefits; this requires in addition advantageous external circumstances, such as light in the case of sight, and good books in the case of the ability to read. In opposition to this, loss of sight and the ability to read *by themselves* suffice to rule out the pleasures of seeing and reading and, thus, their extrinsic disvalue tends to be greater.

Therefore, it seems evolutionarily advantageous for us to be gifted with receptors that enable us to feel unpleasant sensations like pains more acutely than pleasures. This will lead to the elimination of pain as a rule removing something of greater intrinsic disvalue than the intrinsic value of producing pleasure, and it often achieves this by the removal of a cause of greater extrinsic disvalue than the extrinsic value of the cause of pleasure. Obviously, we should not expect any exact match between the intrinsic disvalue of pain and the extrinsic disvalue of its cause, or between the intrinsic value of pleasure and the extrinsic value of its cause.

Now, if for these reasons we have been conditioned to give priority to the reduction of pain to the increment of pleasure, this reaction could surreptitiously carry over to situations in which we compare pains and pleasures that are stipulated to be equal, so that we erroneously judge it to be better to reduce the pains than to increase the pleasures. Illicit extensions of affective and/or conative reactions against our better judgement are known to occur. For instance, arachnophobia is liable to induce in us a fear of small, harmless spiders that would be justified only if they were bigger and harmful, and to make us reluctant to touch even spiders that we know are made out of some innocent material like rubber.

There is, however, a problem with appealing to a tendency of ours to succumb to a slide from the general to the strict negativity bias: it does not explain the discrepancy between intra-personal and inter-personal cases. If we succumb to this tendency in inter-personal cases, why do we not succumb to it in intra-personal cases as well? If we were to do so, by hypothesis, there would not be any discrepancy between these cases. In reply, it might be adduced that in real life it is hard to be absolutely sure that pleasures and pains are equal. It matters less if we mistake a somewhat greater pain to be equal to a pleasure if it is the same individual who will experience both of them than if they will be located in different lives. To play it safe, we may therefore be more inclined to assume in inter-personal cases than in intra-personal cases that the pain is after all somewhat greater than the pleasure, as is usually the case, and be guided by the general negativity principle. But against this explanation it may reasonably be objected that it seems too contrived or elaborate to account for something with the directness of an intuition, though it need not be ruled out that it figures somewhere in the picture.

4.2 Compassion as the Source of the Strict Negativity Bias

We might, however, find another explanation of a strict moral negativity bias if we take into consideration that the psychological asymmetry between positive and negative feelings extends beyond the sensations of pain and pleasure and the suffering and the enjoyment that they normally bring to other kinds of feelings. The negative emotion of *fear* is more widespread and can be considerably more intense than its positive counterpart of *hope* or *longing*. Fear can be intensified to *terror* and *horror*, to which there is no counterpart with respect to hope or longing. As remarked, this is not surprising for life presents more of grave dangers than of golden opportunities. In the case of well-functioning systems like our organisms, there are more ways in which they can be damaged than improved on. We could die at any moment and lose *everything* life has to offer forever, or be seriously crippled and lose a major part of it, but there are no comparable gains in store for us.

For the same reason, *sadness* and *sorrow* can be more intense and long-lasting than their positive counterparts, gladness and joy. *Depression* can be paralyzing and debilitating, but *elation* cannot reach the same pitch or duration. Moreover, in a world in which most of the time we risk losing more than we could reasonably hope to gain, and in which we compete with each other over scarce resources, it promotes our reproductive fitness if the negative reaction of *anger* is more widespread and stronger than its positive counterpart of *gratitude*, since it will generally be more important for us to scare off attackers by displays of harm than to encourage do-gooders by returning favours. Hence, it is not surprising that anger can be stoked up to *fury* and *rage*, while there is nothing corresponding to this intensity in the case of gratitude.

We do not feel gratitude if we receive favours that we deserve, or to which we have rights; if what we receive is positive, it takes receiving more than what is just for us to be grateful, and less if it is negative. Generally, our positive reaction to the justice of states of affairs is weak compared to our negative reaction to injustice. For instance, if nobody deserves anything that is either good or bad for them and, in accordance with justice, nobody has got anything that is either good or bad for them, we are not likely to feel in the least pleased. What makes us pleased is rather the *removal of injustice* by individuals getting what they deserve or what they have rights to (nevertheless our pleasure does not consist merely in the disappearance of displeasure, *pace* Schopenhauer). Likewise, we do not praise people for doing what is just, or morally required, unless this takes such great sacrifices that few manage to do it, but if they act unjustly or morally wrongly, we are quick to blame them.

Finally, that *compassion* with the suffering of individuals is stronger than *sympathetic joy* with their happiness is precisely what we should expect if, as the psychological asymmetry lays down, suffering is usually more intense than happiness. But we should also expect the emotions of compassion and sympathetic joy *themselves*—as opposed to the feelings that form their objects—to be subject to the asymmetry in the sense that we feel more compassion with somebody suffering pain than sympathetic joy with somebody enjoying pleasure, even though on closer inspection we would judge the pleasure and the pain to be equally great. For evolution may have jacked up our sensitivity to the suffering of others in order to ensure that we do not bypass the greater intensity that it is liable to possess.

This view of positive and negative sympathy is anticipated by Smith:

> Pain besides, whether of mind or body, is a more pungent [i.e. forceful] sensation than pleasure, and our sympathy with pain... is generally a

more lively and distinct perception than our sympathy with pleasure, though this last often approaches more nearly... to the natural vivacity of the original passion. (1790: I.iii.1.3)[8]

The reason why the sympathy with pain 'approaches more nearly' the original passion is consistent with what has been adduced here:

> Adversity... necessarily depresses the mind of the sufferer much more below its natural state than prosperity can elevate him above it. The spectator, therefore, must find it much more difficult to sympathize entirely... with his [i.e. the sufferer's] sorrow... than thoroughly to enter into his joy. (1790: I.iii.1.8)

Now if this hypothesis of the relative strength of compassion and sympathetic joy is on the right track, we need not rely on the occurrence of an illicit transmutation of the general negativity bias to account for the strict negativity bias on the Schopenhauerian assumption that compassion and sympathetic joy with others are *moral* emotions, that the reasons they yield are moral reasons. The asymmetry between them would by itself give us the intuition that we have more of a moral reason to reduce suffering than to increase happiness to the same extent.

The hypothesis of a heightened sensitivity to the suffering of individuals has the virtue of being capable of explaining the highlighted discrepancy between intra-personal and inter-personal cases. When we consider scenarios in which we ourselves either undergo both a pleasure and a pain or neither, compassion does not come into operation; we just judge whether the pleasure is great enough to make up for the pain. We adopt the same perspective if the subject of both sensations is another single individual. However, if it is one individual who will feel the pleasure and another the pain, compassion with the latter is evoked—or self-pity if this individual is yourself—and sympathetic joy with the former. Compassion is felt if a subject feels only pain, without any pleasure that cancels it out. Consequently, if our capacity for compassion is greater than our capacity for sympathetic

---

[8] But as regards Smith's remark 'when there is no envy in the case, our propensity to sympathize with joy is much stronger than our propensity to sympathize with sorrow' (1790: I.iii.1.5), I would like to ask 'Even if the latter propensity is not restrained by *schadenfreude*?' In any event, I am skeptical of the truth of Smith's remark.

joy, we might be led to think that letting this individual suffer the pain in order for the other to enjoy pleasure is not justified, even if both sensations are equally intense (and the individual who will have the pleasure is worse off).

If this is the origin of the strict negativity bias, it is hard to see how it could be rational, since a heightened sensitivity to suffering relative to enjoyment could scarcely be rational if the enjoyment is as good for one as the suffering is bad for another. We have seen that pain and suffering are generally more intense than pleasure and enjoyment; so, in general it is rational to feel more compassion than sympathetic joy with others, but this is not so when the pain and suffering are not more intense (or long-lasting) than pleasure and enjoyment. If we feel more compassion even when the pain is not more intense (or long-lasting), this indicates that our capacity to feel compassion is tuned up a bit too much.

We might compare this instance of irrationality to the well-known fact that our fear of losses tends to be greater than our attraction to gains even when we are aware that the losses are no greater than the gains. This is what Daniel Kahneman and Amos Tversky have termed *loss aversion* (see e.g. Kahneman, 2011: 282–6). A simple illustration of loss aversion is that people as a rule demand a significantly higher price to sell an item that they own than they offer to buy the same kind of item. We have come across the exposure effect: the fact that we are disposed to grow attached to things that we get know intimately, so that we prefer them to seemingly indistinguishable things that we do not know intimately.

There may be some justification for such a preference in practice, for we seldom know new specimens as thoroughly as the ones of which we have extensive experience, so it could reasonably be feared that a new specimen will be inferior in inconspicuous ways. But it is not rational to stick to this feeling when we face specimens which we are or should be dead sure differ in no relevant way. The fact that we stick to it all the same is probably due to the fact that evolution has wired us up to have a greater fear of losses than attraction to gains because losses are usually bigger. When we face equal gains and losses, we fail to restrain our greater fear of losses as rationality requires, as we fail to restrain our fear of spiders, open spaces and so on, though we know there is nothing fearful about them.

As we have seen, it is a scaring fact of life, first, that losses are often irreversible, whereas benefits never are. For instance, when we die, we shall be dead forever, being forever excluded from what life has to offer. When we lose a limb, it can scarcely be restored, so we have lost for good the benefits to which it was a necessary means. A disease, if it does not kill us, might mean that we never recover our former good health, but are left disabled, with chronic pain and a lower life-quality in general. The misfortunes that could afflict us are manifold, and they could hit us at any moment, so it is of great importance that we are on our guard against them. In contrast, the gains that we could collect are fewer and will eventually be 'reversed', lost or consumed: whatever assets our genes or fortunate social circumstances have enabled us to acquire, we shall lose them when we die, if not earlier. We may succeed in postponing these losses, and make further acquisitions along the way, but eventually we are destined to suffer the loss of everything.

Secondly, it is also the case that the loss of an ability by itself rules out that we shall enjoy the benefits that its exercise could bring, while acquisition of an ability normally does not by itself ensure that we shall enjoy the benefits that its exercise could bring: advantageous external circumstances are usually also necessary for such enjoyment. To recycle an earlier illustration, if we lose the ability to read, we are deprived of the pleasures of reading, whereas gaining this ability does not guarantee that we shall enjoy the pleasures of reading; in addition, the availability of a good read is indispensable. This fact implies that the extrinsic badness of losing an ability is generally greater than the extrinsic goodness of gaining the ability. If the loss is irreversible as well, which the gain cannot be, the discrepancy as regards extrinsic value widens. So no wonder if evolution has wired us up to be overall more strongly averse to losses than attracted to gains.[9]

My hypothesis is, then, that we exhibit the strict moral negativity bias because we are disposed to feel stronger compassion than

---

[9] In passing, it might be worth observing that a negativity bias could lie behind the familiar claim in medical ethics that there is stronger moral reason to *cure* individuals from diseases, disabilities etc. than to *enhance* their capacities. An objection to this claim is that some instances of enhancement are plausibly no less important, for instance, enhancement of our resistance to certain diseases by vaccination. But notice that enhancement here amounts to the prevention of some sort of harm rather than the production of goodness as is often the case. It might be, then, that the claim about the moral importance of the distinction between curing and enhancing is an inadequate expression of something that is better put in terms of a negativity bias.

sympathetic joy, which we are usually justified in doing, but not in cases in which pain- and pleasure-involving experiences are equal. The difference in respect of intensity between compassion and sympathetic joy in the latter type of situation is an instance of a general psychological asymmetry to the effect that our negative feelings are normally more intense than our positive feelings. As a rule, this asymmetry is justifiable, since negative feelings mark conditions whose extrinsic badness is greater than the extrinsic goodness of conditions marked by positive feelings.

I confess that I am not certain that this debunking explanation of the strict negativity bias is complete and correct in all details, though it seems to me certain that an adequate explanation should refer to the highlighted psychological asymmetry with respect to intensity of feelings; it surely is no coincidence that this psychological asymmetry exists alongside with what apparently is a strict negativity bias. The fact that there is at least in outline a kind of debunking explanation of the strict negativity bias is reassuring, since it is difficult to accept it at face value as a foundation for nw-utilitarianism, in particular in view of the discrepancy between intra-personal and inter-personal cases.

But, as will emerge in 4.3, irrespective of whether this sort of debunking explanation of the strict negativity bias is accepted, the existence of this bias weakens the support for familiar versions of the doctrine known as *prioritarianism* or *the priority view*. The kind of prioritarianism that I have in mind is the *teleological* form as opposed to *deontological* forms (for this distinction, see Parfit, 1995: 8–13 and 20), since I am interested in a form that parallels forms of utilitarianism touched on in this chapter. Teleological prioritarianism declares, roughly, that a benefit to the worse-off has greater moral weight than the same benefit to the better-off, regardless of whether the benefit accrues as the outcome of the acts of moral agents or natural forces. A 'benefit' in the relevant sense need not be anything that is positively good, like pleasure; it could consist in the removal of something intrinsically bad, like pain, which raises the level of well-being.

4.3 The Negativity Bias and Prioritarianism versus Egalitarianism

Let me supply an example of how a negativity bias has seemingly been employed to prop up prioritarianism. In (1995: 35n) Parfit praises

Joseph Raz for putting the difference between egalitarianism and prioritarianism well in these words:

> what makes us care about various inequalities is not the inequality but... the hunger of the hungry, the need of the needy, the suffering of the ill, and so on. The fact that they are worse off in the relevant respect than their neighbours is relevant. But it is relevant not as an independent evil of inequality. Its relevance is in showing that their hunger is greater, their need more pressing, their suffering more hurtful, and therefore our concern for the hungry, the needy, the suffering, and not our concern for equality, makes us give them priority.   (1986: 240)

Notice that Raz talks about bad states, states that arouse our compassion: 'the hunger of the hungry, the need of the needy, the suffering of the ill'. He claims that it is the fact that 'their hunger is greater, their need more pressing, their suffering more hurtful' instead of the fact that they might be worse off than somebody else that 'makes us give them priority'. So, Raz could be read as appealing to a negativity bias, the greater moral urgency of reducing what is bad for individuals rather than to the prioritarian idea of attaching greater moral weight to improving the situation of the worse-off, regardless of whether this improvement consists in directly increasing goodness or reducing badness. Benefits to the worse-off might be thought to have a greater moral weight because they are more likely to consist in reducing what is bad for individuals than boosting what is good.

When prioritarians argue in favour of absolute worseness as opposed to the egalitarian appeal to worseness relative to others as the relevant basis for distribution, they might then be relying on intuitions that could be accounted for by a negativity bias. Contrast the following two kinds of case. If there are individuals who are very badly off, e.g. who are very hungry, there is clearly a strong moral reason to relieve their hunger, which is indeed bad for them. Now it may not be obvious that this reason is strengthened if it is added that there are other individuals who unjustly are less hungry, though egalitarianism implies that this is so. Thus, this kind of case—Case 1—appears to offer some comfort to prioritarians in their argument against egalitarians, but notice that it could just as well be rendered comprehensible by a negativity bias.

Consider instead—Case 2—individuals who are well off but not very well off, say, they have enough wine, but of a rather mediocre reserva sort. The moral reason to increase their enjoyment by providing them with gran reserva wine instead seems quite weak. In opposition to egalitarians, prioritarians maintain that this reason is not amplified by the addition of another population who is unjustly better off by having access to gran reserva wine. But, according to my intuition at least, the egalitarian view that this additional population strengthens the moral case for providing the reserva people with better wine is more plausible. Of course, prioritarians could simply reject this intuition, but it does seem more plausible that when recipients are quite well off and benefiting them consists in injecting intrinsic goodness, it is more difficult to deny that the presence of individuals who are unjustly even better off strengthens the moral reason to benefit those worse off, which otherwise would be quite feeble. Prioritarians would, however, have a hard time explaining why the addition of the better-off population apparently strengthens our moral reason to benefit the worse-off in Case 2.

On the other hand, egalitarians have an explanation of why this—egalitarian—reason is seemingly absent in Case 1 when the worse-off of the two populations are very badly off and benefiting them consists in reducing what is bad, namely that there is a strong reason deriving from a negativity bias which 'drowns' it. Such a bias is not at work in Case 2 because there is nothing intrinsically bad about the condition of the worse-off population here. Even if the negativity bias in play is the strict one, egalitarians could happily refer to it to undercut the apparent support for prioritarianism in Case 1 if it has been given a debunking explanation. On the other hand, it would be awkward for egalitarians no less than for prioritarians to accept a strict negativity bias if it must be construed as evidence for nw-utilitarianism because this view counteracts the positions of both, for example, by advising us to alleviate the pain of the better-off rather than augmenting the pleasure of the worse-off in the cases of the sort introduced in 4.1. Therefore, for adherents of egalitarianism, like myself, it is important both that a strict negativity bias can be debunked and that, even if it is debunked, its existence can be employed to undermine support for prioritarianism.

5
Demandingness as an Objection to Norms

It is a familiar claim that consequentialist types of morality, like utilitarianism, are *more demanding* than types of deontologist morality which feature an *act-omission doctrine* to the effect that it is less hard to justify morally omissions to benefit than actions that harm to the same extent, for instance, less hard to justify omissions to save a life than killing an individual. A consequentialist morality which imposes as strong reasons on us to benefit as not to harm to the same extent is more demanding than a morality which does not do so, by sometimes requiring greater sacrifices of well-being from us in order to comply with its stronger reasons to benefit.

As I have argued elsewhere (2013: ch. 3), the act-omission doctrine as a rule goes with a theory of rights, according to which we have rights to use as we please the psycho-physical powers contained in our bodies and the property we have acquired by means of them. These rights give us permission to omit benefiting others when this would have required spending some of that to which we have rights. On the other hand, others also have rights against us, and this gives rise to more stringent duties or obligations on our part not to kill, steal, and break promises than we would have on consequentialist moralities that deny rights. Imagine, for instance, that you have promised to repay a loan to a wealthy creditor, but that due to circumstances that you could not reasonably have foreseen, your financial situation turns out to be worse at the date of repayment than you expected. A consequentialist morality is then more likely than a deontological morality to hold it to be morally permissible for you to postpone repaying the loan in such situations when you sorely need the money and your creditor does not.

However, if you are well-equipped and have rights to more, you are less likely to have to incur demanding obligations towards others. Consequently, it is particularly for people who have rights to less that a deontological rights-morality will tend to be more demanding, whereas consequentialism tends to be more demanding for those who are better off. I shall soon come back to this point, that how demanding a morality is hinges not only on its content, but also on features of moral agents, with the result that demandingness is demandingness *for certain agents*.

One morality can also be more demanding than another in so far as it bestows an equally high moral status on more individuals rather than lower moral status on some of these individuals. For instance, a morality could supply us with impartial reasons to care as much about the well-being of strangers as the well-being of ourselves and people who are near and dear to us, and to care no less about the well-being of non-human animals than the equal well-being of humans.

Clearly, if one morality differs from another by being more inclusive in the sense of giving more individuals a higher moral status, but they are similar in other respects, e.g. the extension of the class of individuals being capable of acting morally, the first morality is likely to be more demanding than the second.[1] It is for this reason that a morality based on sympathy becomes more demanding when it is required that sympathy be reflective, and grounds like physical attractiveness, perceptual presence and so on are disposed of as grounds for special sympathy. The morality that has been outlined in the present work is more demanding in this way, though I have not argued that it should be consequentialist (as I do in 2013). Similarly, morality as based by Schopenhauer on all-encompassing compassion is demanding (even if we skip the last step to asceticism).

As these illustrations bring out, how demanding a morality is depends not just on its content, on what its norms say about what agents ought to do or not to do; it also depends on matters external to its content such as properties of moral agents, thus it is demandingness

---

[1] I contend that morality is quite inclusive in (2017).

for some agents. A morality is more demanding for some agents than for other agents, since its demandingness depends both on their motivational dispositions and on what is within their power to do to improve matters morally at the time of action.

Accordingly, moral reasons requiring us to sacrifice a lot of our welfare are demanding for us in so far as our altruism is weak relative to our self-interest which urges us to hang on to our welfare rather than spreading it to others, especially individuals who are not close to us. Consequently, a morality that is not demanding for moral saints could well be demanding for ordinary folks.

A morality is also made more demanding for us by the fact that at the time of action we are affluent and well-equipped and, so, in a position to do more rather than less to benefit those who are worse off than us. For as a well-known dictum goes, 'ought' implies 'can'. So, the fact that in the current state of the world there are so many needy individuals that those of us who are better off can do so much to aid renders morality more demanding for us who are better off.

By contrast to the act-omission doctrine, giving up another well-known deontological doctrine, *the doctrine of the double effect*, hardly makes morality more demanding. According to the doctrine of the double effect, it could be impermissible to kill one innocent, non-consenting person *as a means* of, say, saving five lives, while it is permissible to do so as *a foreseen side-effect* of saving five such people.[2] But it is rarely the case that it is necessary for us to kill—either as a means or side-effect—to prevent more individuals from dying, and when we have to kill, it is typically not more demanding to do so as a means than as a side-effect.

Certainly, a morality that requires us to kill *ourselves* no less than strangers as a means to the end of saving several others is thereby more demanding, since killing ourselves consists in surrendering a lot of our well-being, assuming that our future life would be worth living. It would, however, not make morality much more demanding if it is added that you have to kill yourself as a means to an end if it already lays down that you would be obliged to kill yourself as a foreseen side-

---

[2] I discuss the doctrine of the double effect in (2013: ch. 6); see also (2017: 7.4 and 10.2).

effect of this end. Moreover, it would be the fact that this morality does not comprise rights to our own resources which would make this morality demanding rather than the doctrine of the double effect itself.

It should be obvious by now that I am proceeding on the assumption that whether a morality is demanding for us turns on whether it is hard for us to comply with it in the sense that compliance requires *sacrifices of our own welfare or well-being*. When being moral is demanding for us, there is a *conflict or opposition* between moral reasons and reasons of self-interest that tell us to do what is best for ourselves. It would be troublesome for this characterization of moral demandingness if it could be true that we could have a duty towards ourselves to promote our long-term self-interest which could be morally demanding. For it would be paradoxical if the pursuit of our long-term self-interest could require sacrifices of our long-term welfare (or well-being), since it is precisely the objective of our long-term self-interest to secure this welfare. But, as argued in Chapter 2, our reasons to pursue our long-term self-interest are *prudential* rather than moral reasons. The characterization here proposed is meant to capture *moral* demandingness specifically rather than the demandingness of each and every norm. Adherence to a demanding prudential norm necessitates sacrifices of our own *short-term* welfare in order to promote it in the longer term.

Another objection to this characterization of demandingness is that it employs the notion of a sacrifice of our welfare (or well-being), that is, what is good for ourselves. The notion of our welfare is certainly not as clear as we would have wished, but here I have to rely on an intuitive understanding of it, since it would take us too far afield to try to clarify it.[3] My hope is that this understanding is sufficiently lucid to enable us to determine whether the fact that a putative moral requirement is (very) demanding for us could be an objection to its being not justified or valid. I think that the observation that whether a moral requirement is demanding depends on properties of agents such as their motivation and ability to assist indicates that this is not so. This conclusion is buttressed if it is seen that demandingness shares this dependence on matters external to the contents of requirements with other factors that

---

[3] I attempt to do so in (2017: ch. 1).

make it hard for us to comply with requirements, though they involve no sacrifices of welfare.

Consider becoming a vegetarian because you become convinced that the fact that they do not belong to the species *Homo sapiens* does not mean that the suffering of non-human animals matters less. If eating meat and fish does not offer you any particular gustatory pleasure, you might not be sacrificing much, if any, of your well-being by converting to vegetarianism. So, your conversion to vegetarianism is not hard for these reasons. Yet you might, however, find the conversion hard or difficult because your *habit* of eating meat and fish is firm, and most people around you do so, a fact which might appear to make it more excusable for you to do so as well. It takes a certain effort to overcome the force of your food habits and inclination to conform to people around you, to overcome the force of what might be called the moral inertia of going on in the same old rut.

But here the difficulty of compliance is not a matter of having to make sacrifices of welfare as it would be if it meant abstaining from pleasures of the palate; it is a matter of adhering to new convictions. It would be misleading to lump together these different kinds of difficulty of compliance under the single head of compliance being *demanding*. In any case, the fact that sticking to a conviction is difficult or hard because it necessitates breaking behavioural habits and being non-conformist could scarcely be seriously held to be something that impugns the validity or justifiability of the conviction.

The same point may be illustrated in terms of the act-omission doctrine. As remarked, the denial of this doctrine makes morality more demanding because it takes us to have a duty to benefit, e.g. save lives, which is as stringent as our duty to avoid killing, and discharging the former duty is liable to require bigger sacrifices of our welfare in a needful world. But I believe that the denial of this doctrine is also hard to adhere to because it involves a natural conception of responsibility as *based on causation* (as I argue in 2013: chs. 3–6). This conception implies that we have little responsibility for what we let happen by omitting or refraining from acting, since we do not *cause* it to happen. Our *not* doing something, being something non-existent, cannot be a *cause* of anything, something that brings something else about. Now, even if we discover convincing intellectual, philosophical reasons for believing that we could be as responsible for what we let happen as for what we knowingly cause, we are likely to find that we slip back to the spontaneous belief that we are less responsible for what we let happen.

This is another sort of reason why it is hard or difficult for us to live by a rejection of the act-omission doctrine than that this is likely to require greater sacrifices of well-being from us. Surely, it would be misleading to maintain that both of these reasons for hardness of compliance makes rejection of the act-omission doctrine 'demanding', as though there were no important difference between them. In reply, it might be claimed that compliance in both cases requires something like strength of will, but the point is then that the reasons why strength of will is requisite are quite different in the two cases. Furthermore, against the background of these different reasons for which a moral doctrine can be hard to comply with, it appears implausible to assert that hardness of compliance necessarily is an objection to the validity of the doctrine.

Our causally-based sense of responsibility for an event is also diluted when we do causally contribute to the event, but the causal connection between our bodily act and the event is very extended: the more links the causal chain comprises, and the more of causal inputs from other sources than our bodily act that have to feed into the causal chain along the way, the less responsible we feel for its harmful effect. For instance, the causal chain which starts with our carbon dioxide, CO_2, emissions, e.g. by driving or flying has so many links that it takes a very long time for it to issue in harmful effects on the climate. Consequently, it is hard for us to feel responsible for causing this harm. The causal connection between your driving and flying, on the one hand, and harmful climate changes, on the other hand, is obviously far from as direct and perspicuous as it has to be between eating meat and fish and having to kill these animals, so this factor of causal distance may be comparatively insignificant as regards the difficulty of being a consistent vegetarian. By contrast, with respect to climate change, the causal mechanisms are also so obscure and complicated that it is only recently that science has understood them in any detail.

But in the case of cutting back on your CO_2 emissions, just as in the case of vegetarianism, you may also find it hard to keep your newly acquired conviction steadily in mind because you have to resist the pull of your habits, in this case your habits of driving and flying, and of the inclination to conform to the behaviour of people around you. Habitual beliefs are like habitual behaviour: just as when you have decided to kick your habit of biting your fingernails, say, you might find yourself from time to time slipping back into this behaviour surreptitiously, so you might find yourself sliding back to an old belief that you have discovered overwhelming reasons to reject. If the cutbacks that you learn you ought to put into effect are quite modest, living as you learn scarcely merits being called demanding, but they might still be hard to follow for reasons such as the ones mentioned.

The thesis that the demandingness of a principle in the more customary sense of requiring great sacrifices of well-being is no objection to its validity is supported by the fact that for *any* plausible morality there are possible situations in which it would be very demanding in this sense to comply with it. Although it is most improbable, we might end up in a situation in which we have to accept being slowly tortured to death in order to prevent a million or billion unknown people from undergoing the same cruel fate. Any acceptable morality implies that in this situation we ought to accept being tortured to death, even though this is doubtless quite demanding for us in a sense that implies that it is something that it is very hard for us to do because it requires a great sacrifice of our well-being. This is not to deny that a morality which entails that there are *more* situations in which compliance with it requires great sacrifices is *more* demanding.

Schopenhauer puts forward a similar choice to illustrate his claim that egoism is 'colossal': 'if every individual were given the choice between his own destruction and that of the rest of the world, I need not say how the decision would go in the vast majority of cases' (1995: 132). A problem with this illustration is that if 'the rest of the world was destroyed', it is doubtful that your own survival could be any good, if it is at all possible. But his point is clear enough: the egoism of most of us is so powerful that it would be quite difficult for us to accept being slowly tortured to death to prevent a million or even a billion unknown people from suffering the same fate.

Further, if it were an objection to a morality that it was demanding, would it not be an argument in favour of one morality as opposed to another that it was less demanding? Could there not then be a 'race to the bottom' in which moral theories compete to be the least demanding morality? But this seems preposterous.

The great demandingness of the duty to be tortured to death might provide us with an *excuse* were we to shirk discharging it, but this does not mean that we would not be acting wrongly. It means merely that we would not be *blameworthy* for acting wrongly. By contrast, if, strictly speaking, we *cannot* do what it is proposed that we ought to do, this shows that it is not really the case that we ought to do it for, as the slogan goes, 'ought' implies 'can'.

To be sure, we might be tempted to say that we cannot do something if it is very demanding but, if true, this statement cannot employ the 'cannot' which undermines 'ought', i.e. the 'cannot' which implies that we would fail even if we were motivated to try our hardest. Instead, it probably expresses that we are very disinclined to try our hardest. But what we are disinclined to (try to) do should not determine what we ought to (try to) do; it is rather the other way around, that what we ought to (try to) do should determine what we are inclined to (try to) do.

Suppose that if you are willing to let yourself be slowly tortured to death in order to save a million lives from ending in torture, you should press a green button, which you know would send you to the torture chamber, but if you are not willing, you should press a red button, which you know would save you from the torture but lead to the painful death of a million. After considering your reasons, you decide that you are not willing to undergo the torture and, thus, you decide to press the red button, but you press the green button by mistake, with the result that you are tortured to death, and the million lives are saved. The fact that you did press the green button shows that you could do so in the circumstances. That is, you could do what we think that you morally ought, even if you did not do it intentionally for the right reasons. Furthermore, the fact that you decided to press the red button on the basis of reasons shows that your not pressing the green button intentionally is not due to your not possessing the capacity to decide, or form an intention, on the basis of reasons in the present situation. It is due to the fact that your intention was not determined by the morally right reasons, i.e. the reasons that the 'ought' judgement states are the strongest.

It might be objected, however, that this situation is compatible with there being a mechanism in your brain which would have prevented your deciding to push the green button had you been inclined to do so on the basis of reasons, but which was not set off because you were instead inclined to decide to push the red button. Then you could not have decided to push the green button in this situation. True, but imagine also that if this mechanism had been set in motion and had made you decide to push the red button against your inclination, another mechanism would also have been triggered which would have made your hand unsteady so that you would have pushed the green button by mistake. The second mechanism did not come into operation because you decided to push the red button without any interference from the first mechanism, but it is nevertheless true that you pushed the green button by mistake. Then I believe that you have still done what you ought to do, though you have not done so, and could not have done so, intentionally for the right reasons. The fact that you could deliberate on the basis of reasons whether to press the green or the red button, and that as result could have pressed the green button suffice for it to be true that you ought to push this button. Owing to the mechanism whose function it is to prevent your deciding to press the green button, it is not true that you ought to decide to press this button, but it is true that you ought to try or be inclined to make this decision and that you ought to press the green button.

Imagine, however, that you had *known* that the mechanism that would obstruct your deciding to press the green button was lurking in your brain. Then you could *not* deliberate on the basis of reasons about which button to press; your knowledge that you could not avoid pressing the red button would have prevented this. It would not have helped had you known that the second mechanism was also lurking in your brain; you could still not deliberate about which button to press on the basis of your reasons. Then it would not be true even that you ought to try or be inclined to decide to press the green button. Therefore, it is necessary that we can rationally *think* that we can deliberate about what to do on the basis of reasons in order for it to be true that we can do so, and in order for us to be able to consider what we ought.

If you have no way of knowing about the presence of the first mechanism in your brain, you can deliberate on the basis of your reasons about which button to push. As a result, you may try or be inclined to push the green button. The mechanism will in fact prevent your deciding this, but you have nevertheless tried or been inclined to decide what you ought. Moreover, if the second mechanism counteracts this prevention and makes you push the green button, you will have done what you ought to do as well. Certainly, the latter would be true even if you had decided to push the red button without the interference of the first mechanism, but then you would not have tried or been inclined to make the decision that you ought to have tried or been inclined to make.

The conclusion is, therefore, that as long as you are not aware of anything stopping you from deciding to undergo the protracted torture—like an irresistible or uncontrollable desire to avoid it—and there is nothing that blocks the implementation of this decision, you ought to undergo this torture in order to save a million lives. This is true even if there is in fact something stopping you from making this decision.

These observations are relevant to our actual situation, as conceived by Schopenhauer. For he believed that 'the difference of characters is innate and ineradicable', so ethics cannot 'transform the man who is hard-hearted into one who is compassionate' (1995: 187). But our characters belong to the noumenal world, beyond the reach of our knowledge. Therefore, it would seem that we can never know whether our character is so hard-hearted that it will never allow us to act compassionately in the circumstances in which we shall find ourselves. As we experience our failures to act compassionately in one situation after another, the probability will run up that we shall not ever succeed in acting thus, but it cannot reach certainty, since we do not know what our character is like in itself.

If, however, we conjecture that a valid moral norm is so demanding that it is improbable that we shall succeed in complying with it intentionally, we might have reason to try to follow some less demanding norm instead. For the consequences for ourselves and/or others might be disastrous if we vainly try to abide by the more demanding norm. Thus, while the demandingness of a moral norm is no objection to its *validity*—as long as we *can* follow it—it can be an objection to *accepting it* as our guide of conduct. Then, even if we are not blameworthy for failing to comply with the demanding norm, since this would require a sacrifice so big that very few people are prepared to make it, we could be blameworthy for having overestimated our powers of action and having tried to comply with it instead of some less demanding norm when the consequences of failure are dire. Perhaps we could be blameworthy for not having been content with something like what Schopenhauer presents as acting justly.

This raises the question whether it is possible for us to try to abide by other norms than the ones we are convinced are valid. It is plain, however, that we often believe things against our best judgement and act on such beliefs. To take a non-moral example, even though we have every reason to be convinced that we are perfectly safe when we stand behind a fence at the edge of an abyss, we often find the irrational belief that there is some risk that we shall fall creep in on us, and as a result we can scarcely resist taking a step back. Likewise, we have unquenchable, spontaneous beliefs to the effect that we are permitted to give priority to people who are near and dear to us over strangers, as well as to human beings over non-human animals, and that we are much less responsible for what we let happen than for what we cause, as the act-omission doctrine lays down. Thus, imagine that we were to realize on reflection that these doctrines are unjustifiable, but that it would take us sustained effort to extirpate our spontaneous inclination to believe in them. If it were to turn out that it would have deleterious effects were we to try to purge ourselves of these doctrines, we should not do so, but should rather let ourselves go on acting on the basis of them.

Here it should, however, be emphasized that, though the fact that it has good consequences for subjects to have an attitude may justify them *having* the attitude, this is not tantamount to *the attitude itself* being justified, that is, tantamount to *the object* of the attitude—in the present case, the distinction between harmful acts and omissions, or between those individuals who are and are not close, or between human and non-human animals—being such that it makes the attitude in question to this object justified or fitting. Likewise, if it has bad consequences for the subjects who have an attitude, this goes nowhere to showing that its object does not justify it. Smith contends that commiseration for 'the many wretches' 'who are placed altogether out of the sphere of our activity' 'would be perfectly useless, and could serve no other purpose than to render miserable the person who possessed it' (1790: III.iii.8). His being right about the consequences of such commiseration is compatible with the fact that the misery of these 'wretches' still makes it fitting.

If we are allowed to help ourselves to the cognitivist assumption that moral beliefs have truth-value, the distinction could be made sharper. For it then comes out as the distinction between reasons for holding, e.g. the belief that there is a moral difference between acts of harming and omissions to benefit, which support *the truth* of this belief, and reasons which refer to the *good consequences of endorsing* this belief. The latter justification is *pragmatic* or *practical* and has nothing to do with the truth of the belief.[4] It should be conceded, though, that if we are contractualists or constructivists who view morality as the result of human conventions, as the laws of states are, it might be that norms which are very demanding could not qualify as valid moral norms. I regard such views as implausible, but this is not anything that can be argued here.

The general conclusions of this book are that, given that Schopenhauer is right that the basis or source of morality is motivational, he should not have taken this motivation to consist in merely compassion, not even if it is supplemented by sympathetic joy and benevolence, but should have included an independent sense of justice as well. He is right to emphasize compassion in so far as it is stronger than sympathetic joy but, contrary to what he thought, positive feelings are feelings in their own right. His idea that the conception of oneself is involved in compassion for others leads him to postulate a mysterious identification of oneself with others. We should instead deny an assumption that underlies this view, namely that the fact that a person is identical to us is something that makes us specially concerned about this person. Finally, compassion, sympathetic joy, and benevolence, in virtue of the empathy that underpins them, stand in need of being subjected to rational reflection in order to serve as moral guides. This is a process that can be voluntarily undertaken, though it is hard to carry out successfully. However, the fact that an attitude is hard to acquire is no objection to its rational justifiability, though it may be an objection to the rationality of trying to acquire it.

It is, however, not just practical rationality and morality that are excessively demanding. So is philosophy: philosophers have grappled with the big problems of their discipline for at least two and a half

---

[4] I discuss this distinction more fully in (2013: chs. 11.2 and 12.4).

millennia without having attained consensus about solutions to any of them. In all likelihood, they will never attain this goal. It is likewise unlikely that physicists will gain a complete understanding of the universe in physical respects. Or that biologists will learn everything that there is to learn about life-processes, or psychologists about mental phenomena. For better or worse, the world is unfathomable and unmanageable. But it may be more regrettable that we cannot live up to the demandingness of practical rationality and morality than to theoretical demandingness because it means that lives will be worse for us and others than they should be.

References

Aurelius, Marcus (2006) *Meditations*, London: Penguin.
Batson, C. Daniel (2012) 'The Empathy-Altruism Hypothesis: Issues and Implications', in Jean Decety (ed.), *Empathy: From Bench to Bedside*, Cambridge, MA: MIT Press, 41–54.
Batson, C. Daniel (2019) *A Scientific Search for Altruism*, New York: Oxford University Press.
Benatar, David (2006) *Better Never to Have Been*, Oxford: Oxford University Press.
Bloom, Paul (2016) *Against Empathy*, London: Bodley Head.
Cartwright, David (1988) 'Schopenhauer's Compassion and Nietzsche's Pity', *Schopenhauer in der internationalen Diskussion, 69. Schopenhauer Jahrbusch 1988*, Frankfurt am Main: Verlag Waldemar Kramer, 557–67.
Cartwright, David (2008) 'Compassion and Solidarity with Sufferers: The Metaphysics of *Mitleid*', *European Journal of Philosophy*, 16, 292–310.
Cartwright, David (2012) 'Schopenhauer on the Value of Compassion', in Bart Vandenabeele (ed.), *A Companion to Schopenhauer*, Oxford: Blackwell, 249–65.
Coplan, Amy (2011) 'Understanding Empathy: Its Features and Effect', in Amy Coplan and Peter Goldie (eds.), *Empathy*, Oxford: Oxford University Press, 3–18.
Darwall, Stephen (1998) 'Empathy, Sympathy, Care', *Philosophical Studies*, 89, 261–82.
De Waal, Frans (2010) *The Age of Empathy*, London: Souvenir Press.
Hamlyn, D. W. (1980) *Schopenhauer*, London: Routledge & Kegan Paul.
Hare, Richard (1981) *Moral Thinking*, Oxford: Clarendon Press.
Hume, David (1739–40) *A Treatise of Human Nature*, ed. P. H. Nidditch, Oxford: Clarendon Press, 1978.
Hurka, Thomas (2010) 'Asymmetries in Value', *Noûs*, 44, 199–223.
Kahneman, Daniel (2011) *Thinking, Fast and Slow*, London: Allen Lane.
Kristjánsson, Kristján (2005) 'Justice and Desert-Based Emotions', *Philosophical Explorations*, 8, 53–68.
McRae, Emily (2017) 'Empathy, Compassion, and "Exchanging Self and Other", in Indo-Tibetan Buddhism', in Heidi Maibom (ed.), *The Routledge Handbook of the Philosophy of Empathy*, London and New York: Routledge, 123–33.

Magee, Bryan (1983) *The Philosophy of Schopenhauer*, Oxford: Clarendon Press.
Marshall, Colin (2020) 'Schopenhauer on the Content of Compassion', https://doi.org/101111/nous.12330.
Mayerfeld, Jamie (1999) *Suffering and Moral Responsibility*, New York: Oxford University Press.
Moore, G. E. (1903) *Principia Ethica*, Cambridge: Cambridge University Press.
Nagel, Thomas (1986) *The View from Nowhere*, New York: Oxford University Press.
Nussbaum, Martha (2001) *Upheavals of Thought*, New York: Cambridge University Press.
Parfit, Derek (1987) *Reasons and Persons*, reprinted with corrections, Oxford: Clarendon Press.
Parfit, Derek (1995) *Equality or Priority?*, The Lindley Lecture 1991, Lawrence, KS: University of Kansas.
Parfit, Derek (2011) *On What Matters*, vol. 1, Oxford: Oxford University Press.
Parfit, Derek (2012) 'We Are Not Human Beings', *Philosophy*, 87, 5–28.
Parfit, Derek (2017) *On What Matters*, vol. 3, Oxford: Oxford University Press.
Persson, Ingmar (2005) *The Retreat of Reason*, Oxford: Clarendon Press.
Persson, Ingmar (2013) *From Morality to the End of Reason*, Oxford: Oxford University Press.
Persson, Ingmar (2016) 'Parfit on Personal Identity: Its Analysis and (Un)importance', *Theoria*, 82, 148–65.
Persson, Ingmar (2017) *Inclusive Ethics*, Oxford: Oxford University Press.
Persson, Ingmar (2019) *Reasons in Action*, Oxford: Oxford University Press.
Persson, Ingmar (2021) 'Parfit's Reorientation: From Revisionism to Conciliationalism', in Jeff McMahan, Tim Campbell, James Goodrich, and Ketan Ramakrishnan (eds.), *Principles and Persons: The Legacy of Derek Parfit*, Oxford: Oxford University Press.
Persson, Ingmar and Savulescu, Julian (2012) *Unfit for the Future*, Oxford: Oxford University Press.
Popper, Karl (1966) *The Open Society and Its Enemies*, 5th edition, vol. I, London: Routledge & Kegan Paul.
Prinz, Jesse (2011a) 'Is Empathy Necessary for Morality?', in Amy Coplan and Peter Goldie (eds.), *Empathy*, Oxford: Oxford University Press, 211–29.
Prinz, Jesse (2011b) 'Against Empathy', *Southern Journal of Philosophy*, 49, Spindel Suppl., 214–33.
Raz, Joseph (1986) *The Morality of Freedom*, Oxford: Clarendon Press.

Ricard, Matthieu (2015) *Altruism: The Science and Psychology of Kindness*, London: Atlantic Books.
Schopenhauer, Arthur (1966) *The World as Will and Representation*, vols. I & II, trans. E. F. J. Payne, New York: Dover.
Schopenhauer, Arthur (1974) *Parerga and Paralipomena*, vols. I & II, trans. E. F. J. Payne, Oxford: Clarendon Press.
Schopenhauer, Arthur (1995) *On the Basis of Morality*, trans. E. F. J. Payne, Providence, RI: Berghahn Books.
Shapshay, Sandra (2019) *Reconstructing Schopenhauer's Ethics*, New York: Oxford University Press.
Slote, Michael (2007) *The Ethics of Care and Empathy*, New York: Routledge.
Smith, Adam (1790) *The Theory of Moral Sentiments*, 6th edition, ed. D. D. Raphael and A. L. Macfie, The Online Library of Liberty, 2004.
Smith, Richard (2013) *The Joy of Pain*, New York: Oxford University Press.

Index

For the benefit of digital users, indexed terms that span two pages (e.g., 52–53) may, on occasion, appear on only one of those pages.

Act-omission doctrine 93, 113, 125, 129–30, 135
Anger 22–3, 83–4, 117–18
Aurelius, M. 95
Autonomy 44–5

Batson, D. 72–5
  the empathy–altruism hypothesis 73–5
Benatar, D. 115
Benevolence 12–15, 19–20, 25, 27–8, 31–2, 65, 74–6, 81–3, 85–7
Bias towards the future 94
Bias towards the near 39, 42–3, 46, 80
Bias towards the negative, *see* Negativity
Bias towards the perceived 64, 94–5
Bloom, P. 29, 67–72, 76–7, 79, 84–5, 88–91
Buddhism 7, 30, 88–9n.5, 106
Buñuel, L. 79–80n.3
Bystander effect 87

Cartwright, D. 7, 8, 19n.11
Coexisters 38–9, 52–5
  accessed by imagination from outside 39–40, 43, 47
    exceptions to this access 39–40
    obstacles to imagination from outside 40–2, 49–50, 66
  bodily separation of 47–8
  independent will of 28, 47–8
Compassion, (*see also* Schopenhauer) 7–8, 11–14, 19–20, 22, 71–2, 74–6, 86
  stronger than sympathetic joy 17, 29, 118–22
Concern 15, 72, 85–7
Consent 47–8, 53
Copland, A. 9n.5
Curing and enhancing 121n.9

Dali, S. 79–80n.3
Dalton, J. 10
Darwall, S. 16–17
Demandingness of morality 89, 125–31
  as excuse 132
  as pragmatic reason 134–6
  as requiring sacrifice of our well-being 128
  as requiring strength of will 128–31
  consequentialist 125–6
  deontological 125–6
  no objection to its validity 128–31
  relative to agents 126–8
Desert 22–4, 41–2, 48–50
  emotions involving 22–3
De Waal, F. 16n.9, 24, 76, 86–7, 86n.4, 91n.6
Disgust 108–9
Doctrine of the double effect 127

Egalitarianism 24, 112, 123–4
Emotional contagion 16n.10, 69–70, 79n.2, 86, 92
Empathy
  and aggression 84–5, 92
  and habitual action 85
  as imagining feelings 8–14, 68–9, 74, 77–8
  cognitive 71, 76–7
  different conceptions of 16–17, 16nn.9,10, 68–73
  excessive 88–9
  partiality of 28–9, 67–76
  spontaneous and reflective 28–9, 50, 79–83, 89–92
Ethics of care 91–3
Exposure effect 41–3, 49, 120

144 Index

Goodness and badness of pleasures and pains 110–11
Gratitude 22–3, 83–4, 117–18

Hamlyn, D. W. 105n.15
Hare, R. M. 93n.8
Hume, D. 24, 79–80n3
Hurka, T. 111

Imagination 8–12, 77–8
 from the inside and outside 37–40, 53–5, 62–4

Justice and reasons of 2, 5–7, 11, 22–5, 35, 44, 48–52, 66, 83–4, 90

Kahneman, D. 120
Kant, I., *see also* Schopenhauer and Shapshay 7, 56, 61, 92
Kristjánsson, K. 21n.12

Loss aversion 120

Magee, Bryan 59–60
Malice/Malevolence, *see also* Schopenhauer 19–22, 25, 41–2, 65–6, 83–4
Marshall, C. 56n.9
Maximization of welfare, inter-personal and intra-personal 93–4
Mayerfeld, J. 110–14
Mercy/Clemency 22, 92
Moore, G. E. 110–11
Morality
 and prudence 28, 34–5, 37–8, 40, 43–5, 52–4, 93–4, 111–12, 128

Nagel. T. 64n.12
Negativity, bias or asymmetry in favour of 17
 moral 29, 109, 122–3
  general 109, 114, 116–17, 119
  strict 109–14, 116–17, 119–22, 124
  in inter-personal and intra-personal cases 110–14, 116–17, 119–20, 122
 psychological 29, 108–9, 117–19, 121–2
 explanation of 115–16, 120–1
Negatively weighted (nw-)utilitarianism 29, 109–10, 112, 122, 124

Negative utilitarianism 29, 109–10
Nussbaum, M. 12n.7

'Ought' implies 'can' 127, 132–4
Overconfidence bias 51

Pain more intense than pleasure 108–9
Parfit, D. 18, 32–7, 43, 44, 53–4, 61, 122–3
Paternalism 44
Personal identity 32–3, 35–7, 45–6
 reductionism of 34–6
Pity 8, 71
Popper, K. 110
Prinz, J. 29, 68–71, 76–8, 79–80n.3, 85, 87–8, 91
Prioritarianism (priority view) 111n.5, 112, 122–4
Prudence, (*see also* Morality) 34–5, 82, 90–1, 93–4, 128
Psychopaths 85

Raz, J. 123
Reasons
 impartial 32–5, 50–1
 moral 34–5
 of beneficence 34–5, 43, 50–1
 partial 33–5, 50–1
 pragmatic 135–6
 self-interested 32–5
Responsibility, causally based 93n.7, 129–31
Ricard, M. 88–9n.5
Rights 24, 48–9, 51–2, 112–13, 125–6

Schadenfreude 15–17, 19–22, 42
Schopenhauer, A.
 ascetism 98–103
 compassion
  and habitual action 85
  as the basis of morality 1–2, 6, 26, 126
  involving identification 17–19, 26–7, 55–8, 63–5
  transcending spatio-temporal individuation 26, 29–30, 55–6, 61–2, 91–2, 97–100
  two forms of 2–6, 26, 54, 89–90
 consciousness 56–8
 criticism of Kant's ethics 1–3
 eating animals 5

egoism 2–3, 26, 31, 131
    extended 17–18, 26, 60–1, 63
    theoretical 105
eternal justice 61n.11
innate character unchangeable and
    unknown 134
malice, malevolence, and
    schadenfreude 17–22, 65–6
Platonic ideas 56n.9
positive feelings as disappearance of
    negative 7–8, 27, 65–6, 98, 107–8
suicide 101–2
value relative 3–4, 62–3
virtue a means of denial of will 98–105
will in itself/to life 56–60, 99, 102–3
    denial of 29–30, 97–100
    self-denial knowledge-based 105–6
Self-interest/self-concern 28, 31–2,
    36–7, 96–8, 127–8
Self-interested desires/self-regarding
    desires 20, 100–1
Self-renunciation, *see* denial of will
Shapsay, S. 7, 27, 30, 99n.11, 104n.14
    axiological interpretation 61–3
    Kantian interpretation of
        Schopenhauer's ethics 5

Sidgwick, H. 32, 43
Slote, M. 91–3
Smith, A. 2n.3, 8–11, 13, 68–9, 78,
    98n.10, 118–19, 135
Smith, R. 21n.12
Spinoza 95
Sub specie aeternitatis 93–8
Successors 38–40, 42–4, 46–7
    accessed by imagination from
        inside 38–9, 43, 47,
        51–4
    and psychological continuity
        45–7
    obstacles to imagination from
        inside 42–4
Sympathetic joy, (*see also* Sympathy)
    8, 13–14, 27–8, 86, 118
Sympathy 8, 12–16, 19–20, 25,
    27–8, 81–3

Tit-for-tat 22–3, 83–4
Tversky, A. 120

Utilitarianism 29, 91–4, 109–10, 112

Welfare/Well-being 128